Heart Foundation

The
Heart
Foundation
Cookbook

by Sally James

Author: Sally James

Managing Editor: Rachel Blackmore
Editor: Louise Patniotis
Production Manager: Anna Maguire
Design and Production Coordinator/Design: Cheryl Dubyk-Yates
Production Artist: Lulu Dougherty
Production Editor: Sheridan Packer
Editorial and Production Assistant: Heather Straton
Concept Design: Kirsten Farr
Photography: Peter Johnson
Food Stylist: Penny Farrell
Food Stylist's Assistant: Geraldine Ansell
Nutritional Analysis: Rosemary Stanton
Styling Credits: Plates, glasses and accessories shown in
the photographs were kindly supplied by: Gempo Giftware,
Prima Cosa, Waterford Wedgwood and Crabtree & Evelyn.

Published by: R&R Publications Marketing Pty Ltd
(ACN 083 612 579)
12 Edward Street, Brunswick, VIC 3056 Australia
Ph: (03) 9381 2199 Fax: (03) 9381 2689
National Toll Free: 1 800 063 296
on behalf of the National Heart Foundation (ACN 008 419 761).

Produced in Australia by the australian book connection pty ltd
Film separations by: Colour Pacific

Reprinted 1997, 1999, 2001

The Heart Foundation Cookbook
ISBN 0 86455 010 3

AUTHOR'S ACKNOWLEDGMENTS

I would like to thank the following individuals and organisations
for their contribution to this cookbook.
Bev Nicholls and Dorothy James (my tireless mother) for many
hours of hard work and patience testing the recipes.
Members of staff: Glenn Cardwell and Mareeta Grundy for
preparing the nutrition information. Suzanne Newnham and
Michelle Musial for administrative support. Special thanks also
to Robert Hunt, Allan Sharp, Peter Wallace and Brenda Avent
for their support and assistance, to Hounn Ngov for some Asian
cooking tips and to the many 'in-house tasters' whose feedback
was invaluable.

For recipes and ideas:
Mrs Jean Lawton, who spent 20 years as a cardiac nurse in
America and Europe and put all her experience and ideas in a
cookbook, *Recipes For Life*.
Graham Kerr who inspired me with many of his ideas for
bringing flavour and enjoyment into healthy cooking.
Veronica Cuskelly, FLORAfoods; Jan Lenton, Australian Meat
and Livestock Corporation; Annie Foord, NSW Fish Marketing
Authority; Dairy Farmers; Australian Pork Corporation;
Sunrice; Meadow Lea Foods; King Oscar; Sanyo.

 Fisher & Paykel who have generously
provided all the information on freezing
and refrigeration, as well as an incredibly efficient refrigerator
for the recipe development. Look for the **F&P** freezing
information throughout this book.
Ron Bray, The Knife Shop, Canberra, for expert advice and
knives for recipe development.
Medina Executive Apartments . . . the
hotel alternative, for assistance with
apartment accommodation, where all the last-minute testing
took place.
The Observatory Hotel, The Rocks, for very generous,
and pampered, support with accommodation.

Martin Palmer, Martin's Seafoods, for donating the finest
quality fish and seafood for the photography.
Penny Farrell, who managed to create visual masterpieces out
of my recipes, and her dedicated assistant, Geraldine Ansell.
Peter Johnson, whose understanding of the unity between food
and film is truly outstanding.

Heart Foundation

I am pleased to introduce and welcome you to the latest in the Heart Foundation's highly successful series of cookbooks. And thank you for supporting our important work through the purchase of this book.

For many ycars, people have looked to the Heart Foundation for reliable nutrition advice. *The Heart Foundation Cookbook* is for the growing number in the community who are keen to make the most of life through a healthy lifestyle and for those who need guidance in keeping to a low fat but enjoyable diet.

It's time to take a step forward and meet the needs of today's changing lifestyles – how to cook quick and easy meals that also taste great and take advantage of the wealth of fine produce now available in Australia.

Based on simplicity, *The Heart Foundation Cookbook* includes some old favourites made new and some innovative recipes with a multicultural influence. We are sure this book will become your trusted kitchen companion with over 230 beautifully photographed recipes for everyday living and lots of quick tips for meal preparation.

We've also included some answers to common questions about food and health and a chart to help you modify other recipes or replace ingredients that are high in fat.

I hope you will enjoy exploring the pages of this cookbook and the path to an enjoyable and healthy life. Please recommend it to others.

CONTENTS

DID YOU KNOW?

Congratulations on buying this National Heart Foundation cookbook to help you on your journey to better health. As well as more than 230 recipes you will also find information on food and health.

What is cholesterol?

Cholesterol is a fatty substance produced naturally by the body and is found in the blood. It is only a problem when there is too much in the blood. The only cholesterol-containing foods are those of animal origin, however eating these will not necessarily raise your blood cholesterol. The main culprit is saturated fat.

What is wrong with having high blood cholesterol?

Too much cholesterol in the blood causes fatty deposits to build-up in the blood vessels. This makes it harder for blood to flow through them. Sometimes blood vessels can become totally blocked. The gradual blocking of blood vessels in the heart may lead to heart attack. The gradual blocking of blood vessels in the brain may lead to stroke.

What causes high blood cholesterol?

The main causes are:
- Eating too much saturated fat
- Being overweight
- Having a family history of high blood cholesterol

What should my blood cholesterol level be?

The lower the better. Less than 5.5mmol/L is desirable.

How can I lower my blood cholesterol?

The most important factor is to eat a diet low in total fat, especially saturated fat. All the recipes in this book are low in both saturated and total fat. Where fats and oils have been used, they are mainly unsaturated, e.g. olive oil (see chart for more examples). And do not forget to enjoy an active lifestyle.

How much fat is too much?

We all come in different shapes and sizes and have different lifestyles, so your fat needs will vary from day to day. Based on a maximum of 30% of total calories from fat (which is what most health authorities recommend), the following figures give a guide to your own requirements. Use the recipe analysis to help you access your fat intake. (These values are a guide only.)

For the average woman	no more than 68g of fat per day
For the average man	no more than 78g of fat per day

More active people will be able to eat a little more fat as their calorie needs are higher.

For example here is a day's menu using recipes from this book:
Breakfast: Swiss Muesli; Paw Paw Cooler; 1 slice mixed seed bread with jam
Morning Tea: 2 Almond Biscotti
Lunch: Home-style Burger; 1 banana; a glass of juice
Afternoon Tea: 1 Raspberry Muffin
Dinner: Fresh Tomato and Basil Soup; 1 Italian bread roll; Marinara Parcel; Glazed Carrots and Beans; Passionfruit Frozen Yoghurt
Total fat: About 40g
Note: This still allows for milk, spreads and other foods eaten during the day.

How many eggs can I eat?

Eggs can be a quick and nutritious meal. They contain cholesterol and some fat in the yolk, not in the white. If you do not have high blood cholesterol an egg a day as part of a low-fat eating plan is quite acceptable. If your blood cholesterol is high, limit yourself to two egg yolks a week. This quantity is unlikely to affect your blood cholesterol.

Can I eat avocado and nuts?

Yes. Although these both contain fat, the fat is mainly mono- or polyunsaturated. This means they will not raise your blood cholesterol levels, if the other foods you eat are also low in saturated fat. In fact, avocado and nuts contain valuable nutrients that may reduce your risk of heart disease.

Should I be drinking wine or beer?

Alcohol can add to the enjoyment of food. If you normally drink, then limit yourself to a maximum of two standard drinks a day for women or four for men. If you don't drink, there is no need to start. It is far better to eat less saturated fats and to consume plenty of fruits and vegetables than to drink alcohol if you are trying to lower your blood cholesterol.

Can I drink tea or coffee?

Yes. Moderate amounts of coffee and tea can be part of a healthy eating plan.

What are antioxidants?

Antioxidants occur naturally in food. There are many different antioxidants in plant foods such as fruits, nuts, vegetables, whole grains and legumes. Eating foods containing antioxidants has been linked to a lower risk of heart disease and cancer.

Are the recipes in this book suitable for diabetics?

Diabetes is a condition in which blood sugar levels are too high. It is commonly thought that only sugar in the diet raises blood sugar levels. Not so. Carbohydrate foods may influence blood sugars but this doesn't mean that they are bad. Foods high in carbohydrates such as rice, pasta, potatoes, vegetables and fruit are nutritious and should make up most of the foods you eat. Many of the recipes in this book contain carbohydrates, a small amount of which will be sugar. If you have diabetes, you will need to check your blood sugars to see what effect the ingredients in the recipes are having on your sugar levels. Please contact your dietitian if you have any doubts.

What if I want to lose weight?

Despite all the gimmicks, magic potions, wonder drugs, diets and media stories on the topic, the best way to reduce body fat and to lose weight is to eat less fat, and to be more active. For many years, we were told carbohydrates were fattening. It is now known that carbohydrates are an excellent source of nutrients and are unlikely to turn into body fat. However, fatty foods easily become extra body fat. For more advice, get the Heart Foundation's Healthy Weight Guide.

Now relax and enjoy the pleasures of healthy eating.

The key to healthy eating is to enjoy a wide range of nutritious foods. Choose plenty of fresh vegetables and fruit, lots of bread, rice, pasta and grains, low- and reduced-fat dairy foods, fish, lean meat and poultry, and, every so often allow yourself a little indulgence.

FAT FACTS

Fats in food are a mixture of three types – saturated, monounsaturated and poly-unsaturated. Each is found in varying amounts in foods which contain fat. For example, the fat in butter is mainly saturated, while the fat in olive oil is mainly mono-unsaturated, and the fat in safflower oil is mainly polyunsaturated. Remember all fats are high in calories, regardless of the source and should only be eaten in small amounts.

Saturated fats are the bad ones. They can raise blood cholesterol and should be kept to a minimum. Meat fat, high-fat dairy products and many processed foods such as pastries and biscuits all contain saturated fat. Animal fats are mainly saturated, so we advise you to choose lean meats and low-fat dairy foods. Some plant fats, for example, copha or coconut oil, palm oil and many of the vegetable fats and oils used in processed foods are also highly saturated.

Monounsaturated fats do not raise blood cholesterol levels. If your overall diet is low in fat, monounsaturated fats can help lower blood cholesterol levels. Some oils and margarines, avocado, nuts and seeds contain monounsaturated fats.

Polyunsaturated fats can also help lower blood cholesterol if your overall diet is low in fat. Some oils and margarines, nuts, seeds and fish contain polyunsaturated fats.

Trans fats are similar to saturated fats because they tend to raise blood cholesterol when too much is eaten. However, there are only very small amounts of trans fats in Australian foods. Trans fats have been eaten for centuries and are found in small amounts in beef, lamb and dairy foods. There are also small quantities in polyunsaturated margarine.

To lower blood cholesterol levels, limit saturated fats as much as possible:
- trim fat from meat and poultry
- choose low-fat dairy foods
- use poly/monounsaturated margarines and oils **not** butter and solid frying fats
- limit pastries, cakes, biscuits, fatty snack foods and takeaways

A GUIDE TO FAT IN FOOD

Check this table to see how many of the foods you eat regularly are high in saturated fat.

HIGH IN SATURATED FAT	HIGH IN MONOUNSATURATED FAT	HIGH IN POLYUNSATURATED FAT
Butter, lard, ghee, copha, solid frying oil, cooking margarine	Monounsaturated margarine (canola, olive)	Polyunsaturated margarine
Coconut oil, palm oil, palm kernel oil (often used in making commercial foods)	Monounsaturated oils e.g. olive, canola and peanut oils	Polyunsaturated oils e.g. sunflower, safflower and soybean oils
Meat fat, poultry skin	Nuts e.g. cashews, hazelnuts, peanuts and peanut butter	Nuts e.g. walnuts, almonds and brazils
Dairy fat – cheese, cream, full-cream ice-cream, yoghurt and milk	Avocado	Seeds
Commercial biscuits, cakes, pastries and crisps		Fish
Many takeaways and convenience foods		

THE HEALTHY ALTERNATIVES

Changing to a low-fat cooking method and/or changing ingredients by reducing, removing or using something else are easy ways to reduce the fat levels in many of your favourite recipes.

METHOD	LOW-FAT METHOD
Deep fry	Roast in the oven on a lined tray or grill tray. Food can be lightly steamed or microwaved first, or brushed with a little oil for crispness. Crumbed fish and chicken and oven fries can be cooked in the oven.
Shallow fry/saute	Stir-fry using concentrated stock or brush or spray pan lightly with oil. Use a non-stick frying pan.
Roasting meat	Place meat on a rack in a baking dish with 1-2cm of water. For extra flavour add herbs and wine to the water. Make sure the meat doesn't sit in fat.
Casseroles/stews	Trim fat from meat before cooking. Add legumes to add bulk and flavour without fat. After cooking, chill food so fat sets on the surface. Skim fat off before reheating.

INGREDIENT	LOW-FAT ALTERNATIVE
Cream	Evaporated skim milk. Chill before whipping. Whipped ricotta cheese. If desired add a little icing sugar, fruit, low-fat milk or liqueur.
Sour cream	Low-fat yoghurt. Buttermilk. Evaporated skim milk and lemon juice.
Cheese	Use smaller amounts of lower fat varieties, such as mozzarella and bocconcini. A little grated Parmesan cheese instead of grated cheddar gives more flavour and much less is needed. Mix with oats, breadcrumbs or wheat germ for toppings on casseroles, gratins and baked dishes.
Butter/margarine	For spreading use polyunsaturated or monounsaturated margarines instead of butter and spread thinly. Alternately try cottage cheese, mustard or chutney.
Oil	Use smaller quantities and brush or spray pan or use concentrated stocks to saute.
Mayonnaise/dressing	Make your own using ingredients such as low-fat yoghurt, buttermilk, tomato paste, balsamic or other vinegars, lemon juice, ricotta cheese, mustard and fruit pulp. Use no-oil or low-fat dressing.
Meat and poultry	Marinate or add flavour with ingredients such as wine vinegars. Remove fat from meat and skin from poultry before cooking. Sear meat quickly to keep in juices. Keep portions small and bulk up meals with vegetables and legumes, bread, rice or pasta.
Cakes and biscuits	Choose recipes which use less fat and preferably oil or poly/monounsaturated margarine. Sponges, yeast cakes and breads, muffins and scones generally use very little fat and many loaves and moist fruit cakes use fruits and vegetables such as bananas, carrots and pumpkin, or buttermilk to replace some of the fat.
Pastry	Use fillo pastry, brushing every 3-4 layers with oil, juice, low-fat yoghurt or concentrated stock. Use less fat in other pastries, adding ricotta or yoghurt for liquid, or try a scone or yeast dough base.
Coconut cream/milk	Evaporated skim milk and a little coconut essence. Alternatively soak desiccated coconut in warm low-fat milk for 30 minutes then strain, discard the coconut and use the milk.

GETTING STARTED

EQUIPPING THE KITCHEN

Preparing quick, healthy and tasty meals is easier when you have the right equipment. Here are a few basics that will help make healthy cooking enjoyable.

Good quality non-stick cookware: This may cost a little more initially, however, good quality non-stick pans will last longer and greatly reduce the amount of fat needed for cooking. Remember only use wooden or plastic utensils to avoid scratching. A non-stick ridged grill pan is great for searing meat, chicken and fish.

A good set of knives: It is worth investing in quality knives as they will last and they make food preparation so much easier. Don't forget to keep your knives sharp.

A pastry brush or spray oil: These help you control how much oil you use when coating frying pans, baking tins and grills or when brushing food before grilling or roasting.

Non-stick baking paper: Use for lining baking tins and roasting dishes instead of greasing. Also good for lining frying pans when cooking crumbed food. Food can also be wrapped in baking paper for cooking in the microwave or oven.

A wok: If you love Asian flavours, stir-frying requires little or no fat and is quick, tasty and easy. You can also use a non-stick frying pan.

Gravy separator: A measuring jug with a spout that allows you to separate the fat from the flavoursome meat juices after roasting meat.

WHICH OIL?

Here is a quick guide to the basic uses of some of the oils recommended by the National Heart Foundation.

Dressings: Extra virgin or pure olive, nut, mustard seed and light sesame oil. (Only a few drops are needed to add flavour.) Combine with fruit juice or vinegar and mustard.

Stir-frying: Peanut, canola, pure olive or spray oils. A few drops of sesame oil will add extra flavour.

Pan-frying/brushing saute pans and barbecuing: Extra light or pure olive, corn, canola, sunflower, safflower and spray oils.

Baking: Canola, sunflower and extra light olive (or virgin for rich olive flavour) oils.

STOCKING THE PANTRY

Keep a supply of ingredients in the pantry and refrigerator that can quickly add flavour without fat. Here is a list of suggestions to get you started.

A selection of herbs and spices

A range of mustards and chutneys

Several good quality oils (see Which Oil?)

Sesame oil – a few drops give a real Asian flavour boost

Concentrated stocks – look for reduced-salt varieties or make and freeze your own

Tomato paste (no-added-salt)

A selection of vinegars, such as balsamic, rice wine and herb

Dried or canned beans, legumes, split peas

Rice and pasta

Pizza bases or pita bread

Grains such as rolled oats, wheat germ, oat bran, burghul and couscous

Canned fish (no-added-salt varieties)

Canned tomatoes (no-added-salt)

Evaporated and powdered skim milk

Dried fruit, nuts and seeds

Canned and frozen fruit

Tinned and frozen vegetables

Keeping Food Fresh

There's nothing like the flavour and texture of the freshest food to make healthy eating a pleasure. To maintain the quality, safety and nutritional value of food for as long as possible, Fisher & Paykel offer the following tips. Fisher & Paykel have also supplied freezing information for many of the recipes in this book, just look for the F&P tip at the end of recipes.

In the Refrigerator

- Refrigerate foods as soon as possible after purchase.
- Keep the most perishable food like raw meats in the coldest part of the refrigerator.
- Wrap or cover all raw or uncooked foods so that they can't touch or drip on to other foods and contaminate them.
- Cool hot foods before placing in refrigerator.

In the Freezer

- Freeze only good quality food and always remove air from packaging.
- Freeze small, individually packed quantities for easy use. Label with the contents and date.
- If freezing a casserole or soup, stand the dish in iced water to cool it down as fast as possible before sealing and freezing.
- Keep the freezer temperature under -18°C for maximum storage time.
- Thaw frozen food in the refrigerator, rather than leaving on the bench overnight.
- Freezing wholemeal flour, bran, grains and nuts helps delay rancidity.
- Do not freeze salad vegetables, stuffed poultry, cooked egg white, custards and milk puddings, wheat-based sauces or jellied dishes.

Fisher & Paykel
THE INNOVATORS

BREAKFAST

BREAKFAST SMOOTHIES

These quick whip-and-run smoothies make a great start to the day.

Pink Banana Shake: Puree 1 ripe banana, 1 cup orange juice, 6 strawberries and $^1/_3$ cup low-fat berry-flavoured yoghurt.

Fruity Milkshake: Puree 2 cups low-fat milk, $^1/_2$ cup fresh (or drained, canned) apricots, $^1/_2$ cup low-fat natural yoghurt and 1 ripe banana. Stir in pulp of 1 passionfruit before serving.

Meal-in-a-Glass: Puree $^1/_2$ cup low-fat natural yoghurt, 2 teaspoons wheat germ, 4 dates, $^1/_2$ cup strawberries, $^1/_2$ cup chopped paw paw, $^1/_2$ cup chopped rockmelon, $^1/_2$ cup low-fat milk and $^1/_2$ cup ice. You will need a spoon with this one or add more milk.

Paw Paw Cooler: Puree 1 cup fresh paw paw, 1 cup orange juice and $^1/_2$ cup ice.

Tropical Smoothie: Puree $^1/_2$ cup fresh (or drained, canned) pineapple pieces, $^1/_2$ ripe banana, 1 cup low-fat milk and crushed ice.

Orchard Smoothie: Puree 425g canned undrained apricots in natural juice, $^1/_2$ cup unsweetened apple juice, 1 cup low-fat milk and 1 scoop of low-fat ice-cream or frozen yoghurt. Sprinkle with ground nutmeg.

Recipe courtesy of Dairy Farmers

Iced Cappuccino: Puree $1^1/_2$ cups strong black coffee (use decaffeinated if you like) that has been frozen in ice-cube trays, 2 cups low-fat milk, $^1/_2$ cup well-chilled evaporated skim milk, 1 frozen chopped banana and sugar to taste. Sprinkle with ground nutmeg.

BREAKFAST AMBROSIA

Serves 2-3   **neg fat**

1 orange, chopped
1 banana, sliced
1 apple, peeled, cored, chopped
$^1/_2$ cup low-fat natural yoghurt (or cottage cheese)
1-2 teaspoons brown sugar (optional)

Combine fruit and yoghurt in a shallow ovenproof dish. Spread out evenly. Sprinkle with sugar (if using). Cook under a hot grill for 2 minutes or until sugar melts. Serve on toast or over cereal.

SWISS MUESLI

Serves 4   **5g fat per serve**

1 cup rolled oats
2 tablespoons wheat germ
$^1/_2$ cup water
$^1/_4$ cup low-fat milk
1 apple, grated and combined with 1 teaspoon lemon juice
1 tablespoon honey
2 tablespoons sultanas
2 tablespoons sunflower seeds (or chopped almonds)
1 cup fresh fruit of your choice
$^1/_2$ cup low-fat natural yoghurt
ground cinnamon

Combine oats, wheat germ, water, milk, apple, honey, sultanas and sunflower seeds in a bowl. Cover. Refrigerate overnight.

To serve, sprinkle muesli over fruit. Top with yoghurt and sprinkle with cinnamon.

APPLE PORRIDGE

Serves 4   **8.5g fat per serve**

4 cups low-fat milk
2 cups rolled oats (not instant)
$^1/_2$ cup sultanas
1-2 apples, cut into very thin strips
2 teaspoons sunflower seeds

Combine milk, oats, sultanas and apples in a saucepan. Stirring, slowly bring to the boil. Reduce heat. Simmer for 10 minutes or until oats are soft. Serve sprinkled with sunflower seeds. Accompany with fresh fruit and low-fat yoghurt if desired.

Swiss Muesli, Fruity Milkshake, Banana Nut Pancakes (pg 14)

Bubble and Squeak

Serves 4   **2g fat per serve**

1 cup mashed potato
1 cup mashed pumpkin
1 tablespoon chopped fresh parsley
1 tablespoon chopped fresh chives
freshly ground black pepper to taste
2 teaspoons grated Parmesan cheese
1 teaspoon vegetable oil (or vegetable oil spray)

Combine potato, pumpkin, parsley, chives, pepper and cheese. Shape mixture into four patties. Lightly brush or spray a non-stick frying pan with oil. Heat. Add patties. Cook for 2 minutes each side or until brown. Alternatively, cook patties under a hot grill until brown on both sides. Serve on toast with grilled tomatoes.

Banana Nut Pancakes

Makes 10 pancakes   **5.5g fat per pancake**

2 eggs (or egg substitute)
1^1/$_2$ cups buttermilk (or 1 cup low-fat milk)
^{1}/$_2$ cup wholemeal self-raising flour
^{1}/$_2$ cup plain flour
^{1}/$_2$ cup rolled oats
1 tablespoon brown sugar
1 banana, sliced
^{1}/$_4$ cup chopped walnuts
vegetable oil (or vegetable oil spray)

Whisk together eggs and buttermilk. Combine flours, oats and sugar in a bowl. Make a well in the centre. Pour in milk mixture. Mix until just combined. Cover. Refrigerate for 30 minutes. Fold in banana and nuts. Heat a non-stick frying pan. Lightly brush or spray with oil. Cook a few spoonfuls of pancake mixture until bubbles appear on the surface. Turn. Cook until golden on second side. Repeat with remaining pancake mixture.
Serve with lemon juice and low-fat yoghurt, or with jam or honey and ricotta cheese.

Variations: Instead of banana and walnuts try apricots and flaked almonds; peaches and pecans; or kiwi fruit and strawberries.

Ricotta Pear Pancakes: Replace ^{1}/$_2$ cup of the buttermilk with ^{1}/$_2$ cup ricotta cheese. Add 2 chopped fresh (or drained, canned) pears instead of the banana.

Toasted Muesli

Makes 4 cups   **8g fat per ^{1}/$_3$ cup**

2 cups rolled oats
^{1}/$_2$ cup oat bran
^{1}/$_2$ cup unprocessed bran
^{1}/$_4$ cup sunflower seeds
1 tablespoon sesame seeds
^{1}/$_4$ cup chopped walnuts
2 tablespoons flaked (or slivered) almonds
2 tablespoons honey (or maple syrup)
2 tablespoons sunflower (or canola) oil
1 tablespoon linseed
^{1}/$_2$ cup sultanas
^{1}/$_4$ cup sliced dried apricots

Combine oats, oat bran, unprocessed bran, sunflower seeds, sesame seeds, walnuts and almonds in a bowl. Heat honey and oil in a saucepan. Pour over oats mixture. Mix to combine. Spread mixture out evenly on a greased baking tray. Bake at 180°C for 10 minutes. Stir. Bake for 5-10 minutes or until toasted. Cool. Stir in linseed, sultanas and apricots.

Shopping tip: Linseed is available from health food stores and some supermarkets.

Breakfast Omelette

Serves 2   **4.5g fat per serve**

1 egg
1 tablespoon low-fat milk
1 teaspoon chopped fresh parsley
freshly ground black pepper to taste
2 egg whites
1 teaspoon poly/monounsaturated margarine
2 tablespoons finely chopped tomato
1 green shallot, chopped

Whisk together whole egg, milk, parsley and pepper in a bowl. Beat egg whites in a separate bowl until soft peaks form. Fold into egg mixture. Melt half the margarine in a non-stick frying pan. Pour in half the egg mixture. Cook until just set. Scatter half the tomato and shallot over omelette. Cook under a hot grill until just brown. Repeat to make a second omelette. Serve with toast or crusty bread.

Variations: Fill with vegetables such as corn kernels, fresh or canned mushrooms. For a more substantial meal fill with chopped lean meat or chicken; drained, canned fish or low-fat cheese.

TOAST TOPPERS

Here are some great ideas for interesting hot breakfasts or light meals.

Tomato and Onion: Brush a non-stick frying pan with oil. Add chopped onions, tomatoes, chives and parsley. Cook until soft. Serve sprinkled with a little grated Parmesan cheese.

Creamed Mushrooms: Cook chopped green shallots, sliced mushrooms, a little evaporated skim milk and ground black pepper to taste in pan until mushrooms are soft.

Creamy Corn: Heat together canned no-added-salt creamed corn, 1 teaspoon Dijon mustard and finely chopped green capsicum.

Devonshire: Spread toast with cottage (or ricotta) cheese. Top with sliced strawberries, kiwi fruit or peaches. Sprinkle with ground cinnamon (or nutmeg). Cook under a hot grill until heated through.

Peanut Butter and Banana: Spread toast with no-added-salt peanut butter. Top with sliced banana and drizzle with a little honey.

Parmesan cheese is high in fat, however a little adds a real flavour boost and so is often better to use than Cheddar or tasty cheese.

Top: Breakfast Omelette, Paw Paw Cooler (see Breakfast Smoothies pg 12), Breakfast Ambrosia (pg 12), Toasted Muesli
Bottom: Bubble and Squeak, Iced Cappuccino (see Breakfast Smoothies pg 12), Apple Porridge (pg 12)

SNACKS

BURRITOS

Makes 12 burritos   **8.5g fat per burrito**

2 teaspoons olive oil
1 onion, chopped
1 tablespoon ground cumin
1 tablespoon sweet paprika
1 tablespoon ground coriander
500g lean beef mince (or shredded chicken)
2 tablespoons bottled mild taco sauce
420g canned red kidney beans, rinsed
    and drained
6 soft tortillas
12 lettuce leaves, shredded
3 tomatoes, chopped
3 carrots, grated
1 small avocado, chopped
$1/2$ cup low-fat natural yoghurt
$1/2$ cup grated reduced-fat mozzarella cheese

Heat oil in a large non-stick frying pan. Add onion. Cook until soft. Add cumin, paprika and coriander. Cook for 2 minutes. Add mince. Cook, stirring for 5 minutes or until mince is well browned. Use a fork to break up any lumps. Transfer to a bowl. Cool. Cover and refrigerate until cold. Remove and discard fat that sets on the surface.
Heat a non-stick frying pan. Add mince mixture, taco sauce and beans. Cook for 5 minutes or until mixture thickens.
To serve, cut tortillas in half. Divide mince mixture evenly between tortillas. Top with lettuce, tomatoes, carrots, avocado, yoghurt and cheese. Roll up to enclose filling.

When cooking rice, make extra and freeze or refrigerate to have on hand for quick meals, stuffings, patties or for bulking up casseroles and soups.

CHICKEN TORTILLA SHELLS

Makes 10 tortilla cups   **3.5g fat per cup**

1 teaspoon olive oil
2 spring onions, chopped
1 clove garlic, crushed
$1/2$ green capsicum, chopped
2 tablespoons no-added-salt tomato paste
2 skinless chicken breast fillets, thinly sliced
200g canned pinto (or similar) beans, rinsed
    and drained
2 tomatoes, chopped
2 teaspoons dried parsley flakes (or
    1 tablespoon chopped fresh parsley)
2 tablespoons drained, canned reduced-salt
    sweet corn kernels
1 teaspoon chopped fresh chilli (or $1/4$ teaspoon
    chilli powder)
$1/2$ teaspoon ground cumin
freshly ground black pepper to taste
10 round corn (or wheat) tortillas
$1/2$ cup grated reduced-fat mozzarella cheese
$1/2$ cup low-fat natural yoghurt

Heat oil in a non-stick frying pan. Add onions, garlic and capsicum. Cook until onion is soft. Add tomato paste. Cook until mixture changes colour. Add chicken, beans, tomatoes, parsley, corn, chilli, cumin and pepper. Cook for 5 minutes longer. Remove from heat.
Gently press tortillas into 10 greased large muffin pans. Divide chicken mixture between tortilla cups. Sprinkle with cheese. Loosely cover with foil. Bake at 180°C for 10 minutes. Remove foil. Bake for 5 minutes or until shells are crisp and lightly browned. Serve with yoghurt and green salad.

Chicken Tortilla Shells, Burritos

MUFFALETTA

Makes 8 wedges　　　　**9g fat per wedge**

1 cup cooked rice
$1/3$ cup chopped fresh parsley
2 tablespoons grated Parmesan cheese
1 cup (200g) cottage cheese
$1/4$ cup chopped pitted black olives
$1/4$ cup chopped fresh basil
$1^{1}/2$ cups cooked skinless chicken meat
6 sun-dried tomatoes, rehydrated in boiling
　　water, patted dry
1 loaf Italian bread (or cob loaf of your choice)
mustard (or herbed infused olive oil)
2 red capsicums, roasted, peeled, flesh cut
　　into strips
2 large bocconcini, sliced
1 cup grated uncooked pumpkin
$3/4$ cup grated zucchini
freshly ground black pepper to taste

Combine rice, parsley and Parmesan cheese in a bowl. In a separate bowl, combine cottage cheese, olives and basil. Combine chicken and tomatoes in another bowl. Cut the top off the loaf of bread to make a lid. Hollow out centre leaving a 2cm thick shell. Lightly brush inside of loaf with mustard. Place half the capsicum in a layer over the base. Top with bocconcini and pumpkin. Cover with rice mixture. Top with zucchini and chicken mixture. Cover with cottage cheese mixture. Finish with a layer of the remaining capsicum. Press down layers as you go and season with pepper. Replace lid. Wrap loaf tightly in plastic wrap and place a heavy weight on top. Refrigerate overnight. To serve, cut into wedges and accompany with a green salad.

Variations: This recipe can be as simple or exotic as you like. This list of fillings is only a suggestion, any cooked lean meat or poultry, canned fish or vegetables works well. Just make sure the layers are moist enough to hold the filling together.
Cook's tip: To roast capsicums, cut into quarters. Remove seeds. Place skin side up, under a hot grill. Grill until skin blisters. Place in a plastic or paper bag. Stand for 5 minutes. Remove skin. Use as desired.

SALMON PATTIES

Makes 8 patties　　　　**3.5g fat per pattie**

1 large (300g) potato
210g canned no-added-salt red (or pink)
　　salmon, drained, flaked
$1/4$ cup (50g) cottage cheese
2 tablespoons finely chopped Spanish (red) onion
1 tablespoon chopped fresh parsley
1 tablespoon lemon juice
2 tablespoons wholemeal plain flour
$1/4$ cup low-fat milk
packaged breadcrumbs (optional)

Boil or steam potato until just cooked. Drain. Cool. Mash potato. Combine potato, salmon, cottage cheese, onion, parsley, lemon juice, flour and milk in a bowl. Shape mixture into eight patties. Roll in breadcrumbs (if using). Cook patties under a hot grill until well browned and heated through. Alternatively, place patties on a lightly greased baking tray. Bake at 180°C for 15-20 minutes or until brown. Serve on a thick slice of toast or on a burger bun with a lemon wedge and a mixed green salad.

HOME-STYLE BURGERS

Serves 6　　　　**7.5g fat per serve**

400g lean beef mince
$1/2$ cup fresh wholemeal breadcrumbs
　　(preferably made from 1-2 day old bread)
1 tablespoon finely chopped onion
1 tablespoon chutney
1 tablespoon chopped fresh parsley
6 wholegrain bread rolls, split
1 tablespoon tomato relish (or chutney)
6 canned beetroot slices, drained
2 tomatoes, sliced
6 lettuce leaves
6 canned pineapple thins in natural juice, drained
$1/2$ cucumber, thinly sliced

Combine mince, breadcrumbs, onion, chutney and parsley in a bowl. Shape mixture into six patties. Barbecue, grill or cook patties in a non-stick frying pan over high heat for 4 minutes each side or until cooked as desired.

Grill rolls until lightly browned. Spread base of each roll with relish. Top with patties, beetroot, tomatoes, lettuce, pineapple and cucumber. Top with remaining roll half. Serve with a salad.

CRAB AND AVOCADO PARCELS WITH TOMATO YOGHURT SAUCE

Serves 4   **19g fat per serve**

250g canned crab meat, drained
1 avocado, chopped
$1/2$ cup (100g) ricotta cheese
2 teaspoons lemon juice
1 tablespoon no-added-salt tomato sauce
dash Tabasco sauce
8 sheets fillo pastry
vegetable oil for brushing

TOMATO YOGHURT SAUCE
$1/2$ cup low-fat natural yoghurt
2 tablespoons no-added-salt tomato paste
1 teaspoon lemon juice
dash Worcestershire sauce

Combine crab meat, avocado, ricotta cheese, lemon juice, tomato sauce and Tabasco sauce in a bowl. Layer two sheets of pastry on work bench, short ends towards to you. Brush lower half of pastry with a thin layer of oil. Fold pastry in half. Place one-quarter of the crab mixture along one end of the pastry, leaving 3cm on each side to allow for folding. Fold sides over filling. Roll up. Place parcel on a lightly greased baking tray. Repeat with remaining ingredients to make four parcels. Bake at 190-200°C for 20-25 minutes or until golden. Serve with Tomato Yoghurt Sauce and salad.
Sauce: Combine all ingredients in a bowl.

Top: Muffaletta, Salmon Patties, Home-style Burgers
Bottom: Sandwiches (pg 22)

ORIENTAL MANGO CUPS

Serves 4-6   **neg fat**

2 mangoes, chopped
230g canned sliced water chestnuts, drained
2 teaspoons chopped fresh coriander
1/2 Lebanese cucumber, grated
1 teaspoon grated fresh ginger
2 tablespoons low-fat natural yoghurt
6-8 firm lettuce leaves

Combine mangoes, chestnuts, coriander, cucumber, ginger and yoghurt in a bowl. Cover. Refrigerate until ready to serve. Just before serving, spoon mango mixture into lettuce cups.

Cook's tips: The mango filling can be made a day ahead. Store, covered, in the refrigerator until required. When fresh mangoes are unavailable, use well-drained, canned mangoes instead.

HERBED PANCAKES

Serves 6   **4.5g fat per serve**

2 eggs, lightly beaten
2 cups low-fat milk
1 1/2 teaspoons dried mixed herbs
2 cups wholemeal self-raising flour
vegetable oil (or vegetable oil spray)
your choice of filling such as chopped tomato
    or baked beans

Whisk together eggs, milk and herbs. Sift flour into a bowl. Return husks. Make a well in the centre. Pour in egg mixture. Beat until smooth. Heat a non-stick frying pan. Brush or spray with oil. Pour about 1/3 cup of the batter into pan. Cook over low heat until golden. Turn pancake. Cook until second side is golden. Repeat with remaining pancake batter. Keep pancakes warm in a low oven. Spoon desired filling in centre of each pancake. Fold in half. *Recipe courtesy of Dairy Farmers*

F&P: Batter can be stored, covered, in the refrigerator for up to 3 days. Freeze cooked pancakes for up to 2 months.

ORIENTAL CHICKEN OMELETTE WITH PLUM SAUCE

Serves 6   **5g fat per serve**

3 eggs (or suitable egg substitute)
1 teaspoon fish sauce
1/2 teaspoon reduced-salt soy sauce
few drops sesame oil
1 teaspoon chopped fresh coriander
1 green shallot, chopped
1 teaspoon vegetable oil
200g skinless chicken breast (or thigh) fillet,
    thinly sliced
1/2 teaspoon grated fresh ginger
2 cups shredded fresh spinach (or blanched
    bok choy)

PLUM SAUCE
1/2 cup low-salt chicken stock
1 tablespoon lemon juice
1 tablespoon bottled plum sauce
1 teaspoon cornflour blended with
    1 teaspoon water

Whisk together eggs, fish sauce, soy sauce, sesame oil, coriander and shallot.
Heat a non-stick frying pan. Brush with a little of the vegetable oil. Add chicken and ginger. Stir-fry for 5 minutes or until cooked. Add spinach. Stir-fry until just wilted. Remove from pan. Reheat frying pan. Brush with remaining oil. Pour in egg mixture. Cook, without stirring, until omelette just starts to set. Spoon chicken mixture over omelette. Roll up to enclose filling. Serve with plum sauce and steamed rice.
Sauce: Place all ingredients in a small saucepan. Cook, stirring, until sauce boils and thickens.

Variation: For a vegetarian version of this omelette chopped tofu is a tasty alternative to chicken. For added flavour, combine the fish sauce, soy sauce, sesame oil, coriander and shallot and marinate tofu in this mixture for 30 minutes. Drain. Mix marinade with the eggs and proceed as directed in the recipe.

Herbed Pancakes, Oriental Chicken Omelette with Plum Sauce, Oriental Mango Cups, Crab and Avocado Parcels with Tomato Yoghurt Sauce (pg 19)

SANDWICH FILLINGS

Sandwiches are an easy lunch meal for home, work and school. Try different breads such as bagels, rye, sourdough, baguettes, Italian bread or even rice cakes and crispbread. Be creative with fillings and try mustard, chutney, jam, no-added-salt peanut butter, tomato paste, ricotta and cottage cheese instead of butter. Here are some ideas to get your imagaination going.

• Combine cottage cheese, grated carrot, currants, sunflower seeds, parsley and a little orange juice.
• Spread bread with chutney. Top with cooked lean lamb, grated cucumber, chopped fresh mint, lettuce and little low-fat natural yoghurt.
• Spread bread with no-added-salt peanut butter. Top with cottage cheese, pitted dates, chopped red capsicum and celery.
• Spread bread with pesto. Top with roasted capsicum, smoked salmon, baked ricotta cheese, sliced cucumber and snow pea sprouts.
• Spread bread with mustard. Top with lean roast beef, sliced tomato, sprouts and lettuce.
• Spread bread with ricotta cheese. Top with grated zucchini, well-drained, no-added-salt canned salmon (or tuna) and chopped toasted almonds.
• Combine grated reduced-fat mozzarella cheese, shredded cabbage, chopped green capsicum, shredded skinless chicken and sweet corn.
• Spread bread with cranberry sauce. Top with sliced lean roast pork and grated apple, then drizzle with lemon juice.
• Spread bread with cottage cheese. Top with chopped fresh chives, sliced tomatoes, well-drained, reduced-salt canned sardines, sliced Spanish (red) onion and alfalfa sprouts.
• Spread bread with low-fat natural yoghurt. Top with lean roast beef, sliced cucumber, tomatoes, alfalfa sprouts and chopped fresh coriander, then drizzle with chilli sauce.

GRILLED FISH KEBABS

Serves 4   **13.5g fat per serve**

500g firm fish fillets, cut into cubes
juice 1 lemon
2 teaspoons olive oil
freshly ground black pepper to taste
4 large pita (or Lebanese) breads
2 tablespoons hommos (or Eggplant Dip pg 31)
2 tomatoes, thinly sliced
1 small Spanish (red) onion, thinly sliced
shredded lettuce
1 cup Tabbouleh (pg 97)

TAHINI DRESSING
1 tablespoon tahini
1 tablespoon water
2 tablespoons low-fat natural yoghurt
1 tablespoon lemon juice
1 clove garlic, crushed (optional)

Thread fish onto skewers. Combine lemon juice, oil and pepper in a shallow dish. Roll kebabs in mixture to coat. If possible, marinate for 30 minutes. Cook kebabs under a hot grill until just cooked. Alternatively, sear in a hot non-stick frying pan.

Spread pita breads with hommos. Top with tomato, onion, lettuce and Tabbouleh. Remove fish from skewers. Place on pita breads. Drizzle with dressing. Fold in half.
Dressing: Place all ingredients in a bowl. Mix well.

Cook's tips: Tuna, hake, Spanish mackerel or blue-eye cod can be used in this recipe. Hommos and tahini are available from delicatessens, health food stores and some supermarkets. If using bamboo skewers soak them in water for 30 minutes before using, this prevents them burning during cooking.

Spinach and Cheese Pie

Serves 8   **6.5g fat per serve**

1 teaspoon olive oil
$1/2$ onion, chopped
3 mushrooms, sliced
300g English spinach (or silverbeet)
125g low-salt and -fat fetta cheese, crumbled
$1/2$ cup (100g) cottage cheese
2 eggs, lightly beaten
1 teaspoon ground nutmeg
$1/2$ teaspoon freshly ground black pepper
8 sheets fillo pastry
1 egg white, lightly beaten
1 tablespoon sesame seeds

Heat a non-stick frying pan. Brush with a little of the oil. Add onion and mushrooms. Cook until onion is soft. Blanch or steam spinach until just wilted. Squeeze out excess liquid. Combine onion mixture, spinach, fetta cheese, cottage cheese, eggs, nutmeg and pepper in a bowl. Layer 4 sheets of fillo pastry in a 22cm round pie dish. Trim off excess pastry. Spoon spinach mixture into pastry case. Top with remaining pastry. Roll edges to seal. Trim off any excess pastry. Brush top of pie with egg white. Sprinkle with sesame seeds. Bake at 180°C for 20-25 minutes or until golden.

F&P: Can be frozen uncooked for up to 1 month.

Herbed Ricotta Crostini

Makes 8 large pieces   **4.5g fat per piece**

$1^{1}/4$ cups (250g) ricotta cheese
2 tablespoons chopped fresh parsley
2 tablespoons chopped fresh chives (or
    green shallots)
1 tomato, finely chopped
freshly ground black pepper to taste
2 tablespoons chopped fresh basil
dash Tabasco sauce (optional)
1 French bread stick, cut in half lengthways

Combine ricotta cheese, parsley, chives, tomato, pepper, basil and Tabasco sauce (if using) in a bowl.

Spinach and Cheese Pie, Tuna and Bean Bruschetta (pg 24), Herbed Ricotta Crostini, Grilled Fish Kebabs

Bake bread at 200°C for 5-10 minutes or until crisp on the outside. Press centre down slightly or scoop out a little of the bread to make a hollow. Fill with ricotta mixture. Bake for 10 minutes longer or until heated through and lightly browned. Cut bread into pieces. Serve immediately.

Cook's tip: For a change, try using different combinations of herbs – coriander and mint or rosemary and oregano are delicious alternatives.

Variation: For a great meal starter use a cob loaf. After heating, cut off the top and pull out the centre leaving a 2cm thick shell. Fill with ricotta mixture. Replace lid. Bake for 10-15 minutes or until heated through. Place on a large serving plate. To serve, each person breaks off pieces of the crust and lid and dips them into the warm herbed ricotta mixture.

Summer Salmon

Serves 6 as a light meal   **6.5g fat per serve**

450g canned no-added-salt salmon, drained
1 cup low-fat natural yoghurt
1 tablespoon lemon juice
1 green shallot, finely chopped
freshly ground black pepper to taste
2 teaspoons chopped fresh dill
1 cucumber, thinly sliced
1 Spanish (red) onion, thinly sliced

Break salmon into chunks. Place on a serving plate. Combine yoghurt, lemon juice and shallot in a small bowl. Spoon yoghurt mixture over salmon. Sprinkle with pepper. Cover. Chill.

To serve, garnish with dill, sliced cucumber and onion. Accompany with crusty bread and a lettuce salad.

Tuna and Bean Bruschetta

Serves 4   **13g fat per serve**

300g fresh tuna (or well-drained, canned tuna slices in springwater)
300g canned butter beans (cannellini style), rinsed and drained
1 Spanish (red) onion, finely chopped
$1/2$ green capsicum, chopped
$1/4$ cup chopped fresh parsley
freshly ground black pepper to taste
Italian bread
virgin olive oil for brushing
1 clove garlic, cut in half (opitonal)

If using fresh tuna, cook under a hot grill or sear in a hot non-stick frying pan until the flesh just flakes, but the centre is still pink. Stand for 10 minutes. Flake tuna into a bowl. Add beans, onion, capsicum, parsley and pepper. Mix well.

Cut bread into thick slices. Toast both sides. Brush bread with oil, then rub with cut side of garlic (if using). Top with tuna mixture. Serve immediately.

Tuna and Sweet Corn Pie

Serves 8   **4.5g fat per serve**

310g canned no-added-salt creamed corn
$1/2$ cup buttermilk
1 tablespoon vegetable oil
$2^1/2$ cups self-raising flour

Tuna Filling

425g canned tuna in springwater (or no-added-salt salmon), drained and flaked
2 tablespoons no-added-salt tomato paste
1 tablespoon lemon juice
2 tablespoons chopped fresh parsley
2 spring onions, chopped
1 teaspoon fish sauce (optional)
freshly ground black pepper to taste
low-fat milk for brushing

Combine $3/4$ cup of the corn, the buttermilk and oil in a bowl. Sift flour into a large bowl. Make a well in the centre. Pour in corn mixture. Mix to make a soft dough. Knead on a lightly floured surface until smooth. Wrap in plastic wrap. Refrigerate for 30 minutes.

Roll out half of the dough to fit a greased 22cm round pie dish. Gently ease dough into dish. Spoon filling into pastry case. Roll out remaining dough to cover dish. Place over filling. Pinch edges decoratively to seal. Brush with milk. Bake at 180-190°C for 25-30 minutes or until crust is golden and sounds hollow when tapped.

Filling: Combine remaining corn and all the filling ingredients in a bowl.

To reduce salt in high-salt foods such as canned beans, fish and vegetables, smoked salmon, bacon and ham, before using place in a sieve and rinse under cold water, then pat dry with paper towels.

Tuna and Sweet Corn Pie, Summer Salmon

SOUPS & STARTERS

KUMARA BALLS

Makes 20 balls   **1g fat per ball**

400g kumara (orange sweet potato)
1 cup fresh breadcrumbs (preferably made
    from 1-2 day old bread)
2 tablespoons buttermilk (or low-fat natural
    yoghurt)
1 tablespoon chopped fresh dill (or oregano)
1 teaspoon ground cumin
1 teaspoon cracked black peppercorns
$1/4$ cup sunflower seeds

Boil or steam kumara until cooked. Mash. Add breadcrumbs, buttermilk, dill, cumin and peppercorns. Mix to combine. Shape into balls. Roll in sunflower seeds. Place on paper-lined baking trays. Bake at 200-210°C for 20-25 minutes or until golden and crisp.

Cook's tip: If fresh herbs are unavailable use dried instead.

BAKED RICOTTA MUSHROOMS

Makes 10-12   **1.5g fat per mushroom**

$1/2$ cup (100g) ricotta cheese
3 sun-dried tomatoes, rehydrated in boiling
    water, dried and chopped
1 tablespoon finely chopped Spanish (red) onion
1 tablespoon chopped fresh parsley
1 tablespoon chopped fresh chives
freshly ground black pepper to taste
10-12 button mushrooms

Combine ricotta cheese, tomatoes, onion, parsley, chives and pepper in a bowl. Remove stems from mushrooms. Fill mushrooms with ricotta mixture. Place on a paper-lined baking tray. Bake at 180°C for 10-15 minutes or until filling is set and mushrooms cooked.

To make fresh breadcrumbs, place stale bread in a food processor and process to make fine crumbs. Alternatively, rub over the fine holes of a grater.

CURRIED CASHEWS AND POPCORN

Makes 5 cups   **12g fat per $1/2$ cup**

2 egg whites
2 cups raw cashews
1 tablespoon curry powder
1 teaspoon ground cumin
$1/2$ teaspoon cayenne pepper
$1/4$ teaspoon turmeric
1 cup raisins
2 cups plain 'popped' popcorn

Place egg whites in a large bowl. Beat until light and frothy. Add remaining ingredients. Stir until cashews and popcorn are well coated. Spread mixture out evenly on a lightly greased baking tray. Bake at 180°C for 15-20 minutes or until cashews are golden, stirring occasionally. Cool. Store in an airtight container for up to 1 month.

CAESAR'S OYSTER RAGOUT

Serves 2   **3g fat per serve**

6-8 fresh oysters
1 teaspoon virgin olive oil
$1/2$ leek, sliced
1 small tomato, finely chopped
2 tablespoons finely chopped fresh basil
1 tablespoon lemon juice
$1/4$ cup dry sparkling white wine
freshly ground black pepper to taste

Remove oysters from shells. Set aside. Heat oil in a non-stick frying pan or saucepan. Add leek. Cook until soft. Add tomato and basil. Cook for 5 minutes. Stir in lemon juice, wine, oysters and pepper. Bring to boil. Serve immediately with crusty bread.

Cooking with wine can add interest and flavour to a dish and there is no need to worry about the alcohol as it evaporates during cooking.

Curried Cashews and Popcorn, Spicy Lamb Pastries (pg 39),
Kumara Balls, Baked Ricotta Mushrooms

TUNA-FILLED POLENTA CAKES

Makes 14-16 **1g fat per cake**

4 cups low-salt chicken (or vegetable) stock
1 cup polenta

TUNA FILLING

125g canned tuna in springwater, drained,
    flaked
1/4 Lebanese cucumber, finely chopped
1 small Roma tomato, finely chopped
1/2 small mango, finely chopped
2 tablespoons low-fat natural yoghurt
1 teaspoon tomato sauce
1 teaspoon lemon juice
2 teaspoons chopped fresh coriander (or parsley)
1 tablespoon pine nuts
freshly ground black pepper to taste

Place stock in a heavy-based saucepan.
Bring to the boil. Gradually stir in polenta.
Cook, stirring constantly with a wooden
spoon, for 20 minutes or until thick. Pour into
a rinsed 20cm square cake pan. Refrigerate
for 20 minutes or until set. Polenta can be
stored, covered in the refrigerator for up to
2 days at this stage.
Turn out polenta. Cut into 4-6cm squares.
Using a teaspoon or melon baller, make a
small hole in the centre top of each polenta
square – take care to not go through the
base. Spoon a little filling into each hole.
Filling: Combine all ingredients in a bowl.

SALMON PATE IN CUCUMBER

Makes 24-26 **1g fat per piece**

2 telegraph cucumbers
1/2 cup hot water
1 tablespoon gelatine
210g canned no-added-salt red salmon,
    undrained, flaked
4 green shallots, chopped
1/4 cup (50g) ricotta cheese
2 teaspoons lemon juice
freshly ground black pepper to taste
1/2 cup low-fat natural yoghurt
1 tablespoon chopped fresh dill (or 1 teaspoon
    dried dill)

Cut cucumbers in half lengthways. Scoop out
seeds and flesh leaving a thin shell.
Combine hot water and gelatine in a blender.
Process on high speed for 1 minute. Add
salmon, shallots, ricotta cheese, lemon juice
and pepper. Blend for 1 minute. Add yoghurt
and dill. Blend for 30 seconds longer. Pour
into cucumber shells. Refrigerate for several
hours or until set. Just before serving, cut
into 3cm pieces.

SARDINES IN OLIVE PASTRY

Makes 12 pastries **5.5g fat per pastry**

60g poly/monounsaturated margarine, melted
    and cooled
1 cup self-raising flour
1/3 cup low-fat milk, well-chilled
1 tablespoon finely chopped pitted black olives
1 tablespoon chopped fresh parsley
extra low-fat milk for sealing and glazing

SARDINE FILLING

110g canned reduced-salt sardines, drained
    and flaked
1 tablespoon finely chopped onion
1 tablespoon finely chopped pitted black olives
1 tablespoon finely chopped fresh parsley

Combine margarine, flour, milk, olives and
parsley in a bowl. Press mixture together to
form a ball. Wrap in plastic wrap. Refrigerate
for 1 hour.
Divide pastry into 12 even pieces. Press each
piece out to form a 10cm circle. Divide filling
between circles. Brush edges of pastry with
milk. Fold in half and seal with a fork. Brush
top of pastries with milk. Place on a non-stick
or paper-lined baking tray. Bake at 200°C for
25 minutes. Reduce temperature to 180°C.
Bake for 10-15 minutes longer or until golden.
Delicious served warm or cold with Tomato
Sauce (pg 136).
Filling: Combine all ingredients in a bowl.
Recipe courtesy of FLORAfoods

Tuna-filled Polenta Cakes, Sardines in Olive Pastry,
Salmon Pate in Cucumber, Caesar's Oyster Ragout (pg 26)

ROASTED CAPSICUM AND TOMATO DIP

Makes 1 cup   neg fat

2 red capsicums, roasted, peeled
4 semi-dried tomato halves
1 tablespoon balsamic (or red wine) vinegar
1 teaspoon lemon juice
freshly ground black pepper to taste

Place capsicums, tomatoes, vinegar, lemon juice and pepper in a food processor. Process until smooth. If dip is too dry, add a little more vinegar.

Cook's tips: Semi-dried tomato halves are available from delicatessens and selected supermarkets, or you can use Oven-roasted Tomatoes (pg 93). To roast capsicums, see Cook's tip on pg 18.

CARROT AND GINGER DIP

Makes 2 cups   neg fat

1/2 cup red lentils
1 medium (100g) carrot, chopped
1 1/2 cups water
1/2 teaspoon mild curry powder
1 clove garlic, crushed
1 1/2 tablespoons grated fresh ginger
2 tablespoons low-fat natural yoghurt
freshly ground black pepper to taste

Place lentils, carrot, water, curry powder, garlic and ginger in a saucepan. Cover. Simmer for 20 minutes or until carrot is soft. Cool slightly. Place in a food processor. Add yoghurt. Process to combine. Season with pepper. Serve warm with vegetable crudites or melba toast.

To microwave: Decrease the water to 1 1/4 cups. Combine lentils, carrot, water, curry powder, garlic and ginger in a microwavable bowl. Cover. Cook on HIGH (100%) for 12-14 minutes or until carrot is tender. Finish as directed in recipe.
Cook's tip: Fresh ginger can be grated and frozen in cubes.

POPPY SEED CRACKERS

Makes 18 crackers   2g fat per cracker

1 tablespoon olive oil
1 tablespoon low-fat natural yoghurt
1 tablespoon water
1 egg (or egg substitute)
1 cup plain flour
2 tablespoons (25g) poppy seeds
1 teaspoon dried oregano

Combine oil, yoghurt, water and egg. Combine flour, poppy seeds and oregano in a bowl. Make a well in the centre. Pour in yoghurt mixture. Mix to make a dough, adding a little more water if necessary. Knead dough on a lightly floured surface until smooth. Shape into a ball. Wrap in plastic wrap. Refrigerate for 30 minutes. Roll out dough to 2mm thick. Cut into triangles. Place on a lightly greased baking tray. Bake at 200°C for 10-12 minutes or until golden. Cool on a wire rack.

Storage tip: Store crackers in an airtight container for up to 2 weeks.

MUSTARD SESAME STRAWS

Makes about 60 straws   1g fat per straw

2 teaspoons mustard seeds
2 tablespoons sesame seeds
1 tablespoon poppy seeds
1 egg white
2 tablespoons olive oil
6 sheets fillo pastry

Heat a small non-stick frying pan over medium heat. Add mustard, sesame and poppy seeds. Cook until aromatic and mustard seeds begin to 'pop'. Cool. Place egg white and oil in a bowl. Whisk to combine.
Place a sheet of pastry on work bench. Lightly brush half the pastry with egg white mixture. Sprinkle with 1 teaspoon roasted seed mixture. Fold pastry in half, short ends together, to enclose seeds. Brush half the pastry with egg white mixture. Sprinkle with 1/2 teaspoon of seed mixture. Fold in half

again. Brush half the pastry with egg white mixture. Sprinkle with $^1/_4$ teaspoon of seed mixture. Fold in half again. Finally, brush with egg white mixture and sprinkle with another $^1/_4$ teaspoon seed mixture. Cut into 10 short strips. Place on a lightly greased baking tray, leaving about 1cm between each straw. Repeat with remaining pastry, egg white mixture and seed mixture. Bake at 190°C for 8-10 minutes or until crisp and golden. Cool on a wire rack.

Storage tip: Store straws in an airtight container for up to 1 week or freeze for up to 2 months.

EGGPLANT DIP

Makes 1$^1/_2$ cups   **1g fat per tablespoon**

2 large eggplants
1 tablespoon olive oil
1 teaspoon lemon juice
1 tablespoon finely chopped onion
$^1/_2$ teaspoon curry powder
freshly ground black pepper to taste

Pierce eggplants all over with a skewer. Bake at 200°C for 30-40 minutes or until soft. Cool. Peel eggplants. Place in a food processor. Add oil, lemon juice, onion, curry powder and pepper. Process until smooth.

MINTED PEA DIP

Makes 3 cups   **0.5g fat per tablespoon**

2 cups (about 250g) frozen minted peas
2 tablespoons balsamic vinegar (or mint sauce)
$^1/_3$ cup chopped fresh mint
$^1/_2$ cup (100g) ricotta cheese
1 tablespoon lime (or lemon) juice

Boil or steam peas. Drain. Cool. Place peas, vinegar, mint, ricotta cheese and lime juice in a food processor. Process to combine.

Top: Roasted Capsicum and Tomato Dip, Carrot and Ginger Dip, Eggplant Dip, Minted Pea Dip, Mustard Sesame Straws, Poppy Seed Crackers
Bottom: Mexican Bean Dip, Avocado Dip, Homemade Corn Chips (recipes pg 32)

Mexican Bean Dip

Makes 1^1/$_2$ cups **less than 0.5g fat per tablespoon**

1 teaspoon olive oil
^{1}/$_2$ onion, finely chopped
1 clove garlic, crushed
pinch ground cumin
300g canned red kidney beans, rinsed and
    drained
^{1}/$_4$ cup no-added-salt tomato puree
2 tablespoons water
dash Tabasco sauce

Heat oil in a non-stick saucepan. Add onion and garlic. Cook until onion is soft. Add cumin. Cook until fragrant. Add beans, tomato puree, water and Tabasco sauce. Cook, stirring and mashing until a paste consistency forms.

Avocado Dip

Makes 1 cup **5g fat per tablespoon**

1 small tomato, seeded and chopped
dash Tabasco sauce
^{1}/$_2$ small onion, finely chopped
1 tablespoon lemon juice
^{1}/$_2$ cup (100g) ricotta cheese (or low-fat natural
    yoghurt)
1 tablespoon no-added-salt tomato sauce (or
    puree)
1 avocado

Place all ingredients in a bowl or food processor. Mash or process until smooth. Serve with crackers or vegetable sticks or use as a spread instead of butter.

Homemade Corn Chips

Makes 48 **less than 0.5g fat per wedge**

vegetable oil spray (or olive oil)
12 corn (or wheat) tortillas
paprika
cayenne pepper to taste

Lightly spray or brush both sides of each tortilla with oil. Sprinkle one side with paprika and cayenne pepper. Cut into wedges. Place on baking trays. Bake at 200°C for 8-10 minutes or until crisp. Cool. Store in an airtight container for up to 1 month.

Thai Fish and Rice Cakes with Pickled Cucumber

Makes 24 cakes **1g fat per cake**

4 green shallots, chopped
2 cloves garlic, crushed
1 egg, lightly beaten
1 tablespoon chopped fresh coriander
1 tablespoon fish sauce
2 teaspoons sweet chilli sauce
^{1}/$_2$ teaspoon grated lime rind
2 tablespoons lime juice
2.5cm piece lemon grass, finely chopped (or
    1 teaspoon bottled lemon grass)
1 teaspoon cornflour
500g white fish fillets, bones and skin removed
    (e.g. red fish, blue-eye cod or perch)
1 cup cooked jasmine rice
canola (or vegetable) oil

PICKLED CUCUMBER

1 medium cucumber, peeled, seeded
1 tablespoon finely chopped spring onion
^{1}/$_2$ cup white wine vinegar
1 tablespoon sugar
^{1}/$_2$ small fresh red chilli, seeded and finely
    chopped
1 tablespoon chopped fresh coriander

Place first 10 ingredients in a food processor. Process to combine. Add fish and process until just combined (do not overmix or cakes will be tough). Transfer to a bowl. Add rice. Mix to combine. Shape into small patties. Heat 1-2 teaspoons oil in non-stick frying pan. Cook fish cakes in batches until brown on both sides. Drain well on kitchen paper. Alternatively, cook fish cakes under a hot grill until brown on both sides. Serve warm with pickled cucumber.
Pickled Cucumber: Thinly slice cucumber. Place in a bowl. Add remaining ingredients. Mix well. Refrigerate for 30 minutes.

Sesame Chicken Nuggets with Mango Chilli Salsa, Samosas, Steamed Pork Wontons (recipes pg 34); Thai Fish and Rice Cakes with Pickled Cucumber

Sesame Chicken Nuggets with Mango Chilli Salsa

Makes 12-15 nuggets   5.5g fat per nugget

1/3 cup low-fat natural yoghurt
2 tablespoons Dijon mustard
1/2 teaspoons reduced-salt soy sauce
3/4 cup cornflake crumbs, approximately
3/4 cup sesame seeds, approximately
500g skinless chicken breast (or thigh) fillets,
    cut into thick strips

CHILLI MANGO SALSA

1/2 cup chopped mango flesh
juice of 1 lime
1 tablespoon marmalade
1 teaspoon grated fresh ginger
2 teaspoons sweet chilli sauce or to taste
1/4 cup finely chopped green capsicum (or
    cucumber)

Combine yoghurt, mustard and soy sauce in a bowl. Combine cornflake crumbs and sesame seeds in a separate bowl. Roll chicken in yoghurt mixture to coat. Shake away excess mixture. Toss in crumb mixture, pressing on crumbs to coat well.
Place nuggets on a lightly greased baking tray. Bake at 190°C for 20 minutes or until golden. Serve with Chilli Mango Salsa.
Salsa: Place mango in a bowl. Mash. Add remaining ingredients. Mix to combine. Cover. Refrigerate until cold.

Steamed Pork Wontons

Makes 36 wontons   neg fat

2 dried Chinese mushrooms
200g diced lean pork, minced
1 tablespoon finely chopped, drained, canned
    bamboo shoots
1/4 celery stick, blanched and finely chopped
1 green shallot, finely chopped
1 clove garlic, crushed
1 teaspoon grated fresh ginger
1 tablespoon chopped fresh coriander root
1 tablespoon reduced-salt soy sauce
1 tablespoon dry sherry
1 teaspoon sugar
36 wonton wrappers

Pour boiling water over mushrooms. Soak for 10-15 minutes or until soft. Drain. Remove and discard stems. Finely chop. Combine mushrooms, pork, bamboo shoots, celery, shallot, garlic, ginger, coriander, soy sauce, sherry and sugar in a bowl. Cover. Refrigerate for 30 minutes.
Place a spoonful of the pork mixture in the centre of each wonton wrapper. Brush edges with water. Draw corners together and twist to seal. Cover a large saucepan of boiling water with a bamboo or metal steamer. Place wontons in steamer. Steam for 5 minutes or until cooked.

Cook's tip: Keep wonton wrappers under a damp tea towel to prevent drying out.

Samosas

Makes 16 samosas   4g fat per samosa

1 teaspoon vegetable oil
2 onions, finely chopped
1 clove garlic chopped
1 teaspoon grated fresh ginger
1 tablespoon curry powder
1 tablespoon lemon juice
250g lean beef mince
1/4 cup hot water
2 tablespoons chopped fresh mint
8 sheets fillo pastry
2 tablespoons vegetable oil, extra

Heat oil in a non-stick frying pan. Add onions, garlic and ginger. Cook until onions are soft. Add curry powder, lemon juice and mince. Cook until mince is browned. Add water. Simmer, uncovered, until liquid evaporates. Stir in mint. Cool.
Layer 2 sheets of pastry. Brush with a little of the extra oil. Cut pastry lengthways into 4 strips. Place a spoonful of beef mixture on one end of each strip. Fold one corner end of pastry diagonally over filling to form a triangle. Continue folding corner to corner and retaining triangular shape. Repeat with remaining pastry, oil and filling. Place on lightly greased baking trays. Bake at 180°C for 10-12 minutes or until golden.

Kumara and Apple Soup

Serves 8   **0.5g fat per serve**

1kg kumara (orange sweet potato), chopped
2 green apples, peeled and chopped
2 onions, chopped
2 sticks celery, chopped
1 teaspoon ground cumin
freshly ground black pepper to taste
6 cups low-salt chicken stock

Place all ingredients in a saucepan. Bring to the boil. Cover. Reduce heat. Simmer for 30 minutes or until vegetables are very soft. Cool slightly. Place in a food processor. Process until smooth. Return to saucepan. Reheat. Serve with crusty bread or rolls.

Chicken and Corn Soup

Serves 6   **5g fat per serve**

1 tablespoon vegetable oil
4 green shallots, chopped
1 teaspoon grated fresh ginger
1 potato, chopped
6 cups low-salt chicken stock
1 teaspoon dried mixed herbs
1 cup chopped cooked skinless chicken
270g canned reduced-salt sweet corn kernels, drained
freshly ground black pepper to taste

Heat oil in a saucepan. Add shallots and ginger. Cook until shallots are soft. Add potato, stock and herbs. Bring to the boil. Reduce heat. Simmer for 10-15 minutes or until potato is tender. Cool slightly. Place in a food processor. Process until smooth. Return to pan. Stir in chicken and corn. Cook over low heat until heated. Season with pepper. Serve with crusty bread.

Seafood Chowder

Serves 6   **2.5g fat per serve**

2½ cups water
500g boneless fish fillets and mixed seafood
   (e.g. scallops, oysters, clams and mussels)
1 cup chopped carrot
1 cup chopped potato

Seafood Chowder, Chicken and Corn Soup, Kumara and Apple Soup, Broccoli and Carrot Soup (pg 36)

½ cup chopped red capsicum
½ cup sliced onion
1 cup chopped celery
½ cup plain flour
1½ cups evaporated skim milk (or low-fat milk)
1 tablespoon chopped fresh parsley (or fennel)
freshly ground black pepper to taste

Bring water to the boil in a saucepan. Add fish and seafood. Simmer for 5-10 minutes or until cooked. Remove from water. Chop seafood and flake fish. Add carrot, potato, capsicum, onion and celery to stock. Bring to the boil. Reduce heat. Simmer until potato is just cooked. Blend flour with milk. Remove soup from heat. Stir in flour mixture. Cook, stirring, until soup boils and thickens slightly. Return fish and seafood to pan. Stir in parsley. Season with pepper. Serve with warm bread rolls.

BROCCOLI AND CARROT SOUP

Serves 6　　　　　　**4g fat per serve**

1 tablespoon poly/monounsaturated margarine
1 onion, chopped
1 large carrot, chopped
400g broccoli, chopped
3 cups low-salt vegetable (or chicken) stock
1 cup low-fat milk
1/4 cup oat bran

Melt margarine in a saucepan. Add onion. Cook until soft. Add carrot. Cook, stirring, for 1 minute. Add broccoli and stock. Bring to the boil. Cover. Simmer for 15 minutes or until vegetables are soft. Cool slightly. Place in a food processor. Process until smooth. Return to saucepan. Stir in milk and oat bran. Simmer for 2 minutes. *Recipe courtesy of Dairy Farmers, Farmers Best milk*

CREAMY POTATO AND PESTO SOUP

Serves 6　　　　　　**9.5g fat per serve**

1 tablespoon olive oil
500g potato, peeled and chopped
1 clove garlic
1 tablespoon fresh thyme (or 1 teaspoon dried thyme)
1 cup low-fat milk
1 1/2 cups low-salt chicken stock
freshly ground black pepper to taste

PESTO
1/2 cup chopped fresh parsley
1/2 cup chopped fresh basil
1/4 cup pine nuts
1 tablespoon grated Parmesan cheese
2 teaspoons olive oil
2 tablespoons lemon juice
1/4 cup boiling water

Heat oil in a saucepan. Add potato, garlic and thyme. Cook, stirring, for 3 minutes. Stir in milk, stock and pepper. Bring to the boil. Reduce heat. Simmer for 30 minutes or until potatoes are cooked. Cool slightly. Place in a food processor. Process until smooth. Return to saucepan. Heat. Serve topped with pesto.

Pesto: Puree all ingredients, except water in a food processor. Just before serving, stir in boiling water.

FRESH TOMATO AND BASIL SOUP

Serves 6　　　　　　**3.5g fat per serve**

1 tablespoon olive oil
1 small onion, chopped
1 clove garlic, crushed
1 carrot, chopped
1 stick celery, chopped
2 tablespoons no-added-salt tomato paste
2 cups chopped fresh peeled tomatoes (or 425g canned no-added-salt tomatoes)
2 cups low-salt chicken stock
2 tablespoons chopped fresh basil (or 1 teaspoon dried basil)
1/2 teaspoon dried mixed herbs
juice of 1 lemon
freshly ground black pepper to taste

Heat oil in a saucepan. Add onion, garlic, carrot and celery. Cook for 3 minutes. Stir in tomato paste. Add remaining ingredients. Simmer, uncovered, for 30 minutes or until vegetables are soft. Cool slightly. Place in food processor. Process until smooth. Return to saucepan. Reheat. Serve topped with low-fat natural yoghurt.

CHILLED AVOCADO SOUP

Serves 8　　　　　　**17g fat per serve**

2 large (or 3 medium) ripe avocados, halved, stoned
juice of 1 lemon
2 1/2 cups low-salt chicken stock
2/3 cup low-fat natural yoghurt
freshly ground black pepper to taste
fresh chives
fresh parsley sprigs

Place avocado flesh, lemon juice, stock, yoghurt and pepper in food processor. Process until smooth. Cover. Refrigerate until well chilled. Serve soup sprinkled with chives and parsley.

Creamy Potato and Pesto Soup, Minestrone (pg 38), Chilled Avocado Soup, Fresh Tomato and Basil Soup

CAULIFLOWER AND LEEK SOUP WITH SPICED YOGHURT

Serves 6   **2.5g fat per serve**

2 teaspoons olive oil
3 leeks, chopped
1/2 medium cauliflower, chopped
4 cups low-salt chicken stock
1 teaspoon dried sage (or thyme)
1 teaspoon dried rosemary
2 tablespoons lemon juice
1/2 teaspoon black pepper
1 tablespoon chopped fresh chives

SPICED YOGHURT
1/2 cup low-fat natural yoghurt
1 teaspoon lemon juice
1/2 teaspoon ground cumin
1/4 teaspoon turmeric
1/4 teaspoon mild curry paste

Heat oil in a saucepan. Add leeks. Cook until soft. Add remaining soup ingredients except chives. Bring to the boil. Reduce heat. Simmer for 30 minutes or until cauliflower is tender. Cool slightly. Place in a food processor. Process until smooth. Return to saucepan. Reheat. To serve, top with a spoonful of Spiced Yoghurt and sprinkle with chives.
Spiced Yoghurt: Combine all ingredients.

PUMPKIN SOUP

Serves 6   **4.5g fat per serve**

2 teaspoons poly/monounsaturated margarine
250g chopped leeks
3 cups low-salt chicken stock
500g pumpkin, seeds removed and roasted, flesh chopped
freshly ground black pepper to taste
low-fat honey yoghurt to serve

CROUTONS
3 slices brown bread
2-3 teaspoons vegetable oil

Melt margarine in a saucepan. Add leeks. Cover. Cook over low heat for 10 minutes or until soft. Add stock and pumpkin flesh. Cover. Simmer, for 20 minutes or until pumpkin is cooked. Cool slightly. Place in a food processor. Process until smooth. Return to saucepan. Reheat. Season with pepper. To serve, top with yoghurt and scatter with croutons and roasted pumpkin seeds.
Croutons: Lightly brush both sides of bread with oil. Place on a baking tray. Bake at 180°C for 10-15 minutes or until crisp. Cut into small cubes.

MINESTRONE

Serves 4   **4g fat per serve**

1 teaspoon olive oil
1 onion, chopped
250g pasta shells
2 carrots, chopped
2 sticks celery, chopped
1 red capsicum, chopped
100g cauliflower, chopped
100g broccoli, chopped
425g canned no-added-salt tomatoes
2 tablespoons chopped fresh basil
4 cups low-salt chicken stock
420g canned red kidney beans, rinsed and drained
1 tablespoon fresh Parmesan cheese shavings

Heat oil in a saucepan. Add onion. Cook until soft. Add next 9 ingredients. Bring to the boil. Reduce heat. Simmer for 15 minutes or until pasta and vegetables are tender. Add beans. Simmer for 5 minutes longer. To serve, top with Parmesan cheese shavings and accompany with Italian bread.

FRESH ASPARAGUS SOUP

Serves 4   **3g fat per serve**

2 teaspoons vegetable oil
1/2 onion, chopped
1 clove garlic, crushed
1 teaspoon chopped fresh chives
1 tablespoon plain flour
freshly ground black pepper to taste
500g fresh asparagus spears, sliced (reserve 12 tips for garnish)
1 1/3 cups low-salt chicken stock
1 teaspoon grated lemon rind
1/4 cup evaporated skim milk

Heat oil in a saucepan. Add onion, garlic and chives. Cook until onion is soft. Add flour and pepper. Cook, stirring, until mixture is dry and grainy. Add asparagus, stock and lemon rind. Bring to the boil. Reduce heat. Simmer, uncovered, until asparagus is just tender. Cool slightly. Place in a food processor. Process until smooth. Return to saucepan. Stir in milk. Reheat gently. Blanch reserved aspasragus tips. Serve soup garnished with blanched asparagus tips.

SPICY LAMB PASTRIES

Makes 24 pastries   **3g fat per pastry**

$^1/_2$ cup sultanas, chopped
500g lean lamb fillets, trimmed of all visible fat, chopped (or very lean lamb mince)
2 teaspoons ground cumin
1 teaspoon ground cinnamon
$^1/_2$ teaspoon ground allspice
2 tablespoons olive oil
1 onion, finely chopped
1 clove garlic, crushed
$^1/_4$ cup low-salt chicken stock
2 tablespoons pine nuts, lightly toasted
$^1/_4$ cup chopped fresh parsley
1 tablespoon chopped fresh mint
1 tablespoon no-added-salt tomato paste
grated rind and juice of 1 lemon
freshly ground black pepper to taste
1 egg white
8 sheets fillo pastry
1 teaspoon sesame seeds

Soak sultanas in boiling water for 5 minutes. Drain well. Process lamb in a food processor until coarsely ground. Add cumin, cinnamon and allspice. Process to combine. Heat 2 teaspoons of the oil in a non-stick frying pan. Add onion and garlic. Cook until onion is soft. Add lamb mixture. Cook, stirring, until lamb is browned. Drain off any excess fat. Add sultanas, stock, pine nuts, parsley, mint, tomato paste and lemon rind and juice. Cook over low heat for 2 minutes or until liquid is absorbed. Season with pepper. Cool. Whisk together egg white and remaining oil. Cut a sheet of pastry into 3 strips,

Fresh Asparagus Soup, Pumpkin Soup, Cauliflower and Leek Soup with Spiced Yoghurt

lengthways. Brush half of each strip with egg white mixture. Fold each strip in half. Brush again with egg white mixture. Place 1 tablespoon lamb mixture along shortest end of each pastry strip leaving 1cm on each side. Fold in sides. Roll to enclose filling. Place pastries on a lightly greased baking tray. Repeat with remaining pastry, egg white mixture and lamb mixture. Brush pastries with remaining egg white mixture. Sprinkle with sesame seeds. Bake at 180°C for 20-25 minutes or until crisp and golden.

When using fillo pastry, to prevent it from drying out, cover with a damp tea towel. Brushing every second or third sheet of pastry with oil will result in crisper and browner pastry, but it is not essential.

FISH

ORIENTAL GLAZED FISH

Serves 4   **6g fat per serve**

2 tablespoons dry sherry
1 teaspoon reduced-salt soy sauce
1/4 teaspoon five spice powder, optional
1 teaspoon grated fresh ginger
1 tablespoon hoisin (or plum) sauce
1/2 teaspoon sesame oil
1 teaspoon honey
1 tablespoon sesame seeds
4 (about 500g) fish fillets (e.g. tuna, ocean
    trout, Spanish mackerel, warehou, bream,
    snapper, gemfish, red emperor, mahi mahi
    or blue-eye cod), skin and bones removed

Combine all ingredients except fish in a bowl. Add fish. Turn to coat. Transfer fish to a lightly oiled baking dish. Bake at 190°C for 15-20 minutes or until cooked. Alternatively, cook under a hot grill for 3-4 minutes each side, brushing several times with marinade. Serve on a bed of rice with steamed bok choy, red capsicum or stir-fried vegetables.

GARLIC PRAWNS AND RICE

Serves 6   **4g fat per serve**

1 tablespoon peanut (or canola) oil
1 onion, cut into 8 wedges
2-3 cloves garlic, chopped
2 teaspoons chopped fresh ginger
1 small fresh red chilli, chopped
500g peeled uncooked (green) prawns
1/2 cup drained, canned sliced bamboo shoots
1/2 green capsicum, thinly sliced
1 tablespoon fish sauce
1 tablespoon sweet chilli sauce
2 teaspoons reduced-salt soy sauce
1/4 cup water
1 teaspoon cornflour
2 cups fragrant jasmine rice
fresh basil leaves

Heat oil in a wok. Add onion, garlic, ginger and chilli. Stir-fry for 2-3 minutes. Add prawns. Stir-fry until they change colour.

Add bamboo shoots and capsicum. Stir-fry for 1 minute. Combine fish sauce, chilli sauce, soy sauce, water and cornflour. Stir into pan. Cook until mixture boils and thickens. Boil or steam rice. Drain well.

To serve, spoon prawns over rice and garnish with basil leaves.

REDFISH ROLLS

Serves 4   **11.5g fat per serve**

1/3 cup burghul
1/3 cup grated carrot
1 tablespoon chopped fresh parsley
1/4 cup chopped roasted macadamia nuts (or
    pine nuts)
1/2 cup cooked rice
1 green shallot, chopped
grated rind and juice of 1 lemon
8 (about 500g) redfish (small flathead, bream
    or trevally) fillets, skin and bones removed
1/2 cup dry white wine
1/4 cup low-fat milk
freshly ground black pepper to taste
1-2 teaspoons grated Parmesan cheese

Place burghul in a bowl. Pour over boiling water to cover. Stand for 20 minutes. Drain well. Combine 1/4 cup of the burghul, the carrot, parsley, 2 tablespoons nuts, rice, shallot and lemon rind and juice in a bowl. Place fish skinned side up on work bench. Divide rice mixture into 8 portions. Place one portion of rice mixture on one end of each fillet. Roll up. Secure with wooden toothpicks. Place in an 18-20cm casserole dish. Pour over wine and milk. Sprinkle with pepper. Combine remaining nuts, burghul and Parmesan cheese. Sprinkle over rolls. Bake at 180°C for 15-20 minutes or until fish is cooked. Serve with steamed vegetables or green salad.

Oriental Glazed Fish, Warm Balsamic
Fish Salad (pg 44), Garlic Prawns and Rice

FISH POACHED IN WINE

Serves 4   **3.5g fat per serve**

juice of 1 large lemon
1/2 cup dry white wine
2 green shallots, sliced
4 (about 500g) fish fillets (e.g. trevally, John dory, snapper, salmon, red emperor or ocean perch)
freshly ground black pepper to taste
2 teaspoons chopped fresh parsley
1/2 teaspoon dried oregano (or 1 teaspoon chopped fresh oregano)
1 lemon, thinly sliced
8-12 fresh asparagus spears, halved
10 English spinach leaves

Heat lemon juice and wine in a straight-sided shallow pan. Add shallots. Cook over low heat for 1-2 minutes. Add fish. Sprinkle with pepper, parsley and oregano. Top with lemon slices. Cover. Simmer for 3 minutes. Scatter asparagus and spinach around fish. Cover. Simmer for 3-4 minutes or until fish is cooked. Remove fish and vegetables from pan. Keep warm. Bring liquid remaining in pan to the boil. Boil for 5-6 minutes or until sauce reduces and thickens. To serve, spoon sauce over fish and accompany with steamed vegetables of your choice.

MACADAMIA-CRUSTED MACKEREL

Serves 4   **16g fat per serve**

1 tablespoon lemon (or lime) juice
2 teaspoons macadamia (or virgin olive) oil
1 tablespoon wholegrain (or Dijon) mustard
4 (about 500g) Spanish mackerel (salmon, blue-eye cod, barramundi, flake, swordfish or mahi mahi) fillets, skin and bones removed
freshly ground black pepper to taste
1/3 cup finely chopped macadamia nuts
1/2 teaspoon dried basil
1 teaspoon dried oregano

Combine lemon juice, oil and mustard. Brush over fish. Sprinkle with pepper. Combine nuts, basil and oregano in a large flat dish. Roll fish in mixture to coat well. Place in a baking dish. Bake at 190°C for 10-15 minutes or until cooked. Serve on a bed of lettuce accompanied by crusty bread and Yoghurt Cucumber Sauce (pg 136).

SALMON BAKED IN PAPER WITH ROASTED CAPSICUM SAUCE

Serves 4   **4.5g fat per serve**

4 (about 500g) salmon (ocean trout, perch, Spanish mackerel or John dory) fillets, skin and bones removed
freshly ground black pepper to taste
2 tablespoons lime (or lemon) juice
100g salmon trimmings, skin and bones removed (or uncooked prawn meat)
2 tablespoons low-fat natural yoghurt (or ricotta cheese)
1 egg white
2 teaspoons chopped fresh parsley (or coriander)
1 teaspoon chopped fresh dill

ROASTED CAPSICUM SAUCE

2 red capsicums, roasted and chopped
1 tablespoon red wine vinegar
1 tablespoon champagne (or white wine) vinegar
freshly ground black pepper to taste

Place each fillet in the centre of a 40cm square piece of baking paper. Sprinkle with pepper and lime juice. Place salmon trimmings in a food processor. Process to make a fine paste. Add remaining ingredients. Using the pulse button process to combine. Spoon one-quarter of the pureed mixture onto each salmon fillet. Fold paper over to enclose fillets. Place parcels on a baking tray. Bake at 180-190°C for 8-10 minutes or until cooked. Serve with Roasted Capsicum Sauce and Hazelnut Rice Salad (pg 96).
Sauce: Puree all ingredients in a food processor.

Fish in Fillo Pastry: To make completely edible parcels use 2 sheets of fillo pastry for each parcel instead of the baking paper.

Macadamia-crusted Mackerel, Hazelnut Rice Salad (pg 96),
Salmon Baked in Paper with Roasted Capsicum Sauce,
Seared Tuna with Parsnip Puree (pg 47)

THAI-STYLE BLUE-EYE COD

Serves 6   **3g fat per serve**

2 teaspoons vegetable oil
1 large onion, sliced
2 teaspoons grated fresh ginger
2 cloves garlic, crushed
1 small fresh red chilli, seeded and chopped
1 red capsicum, chopped
2 tablespoons chopped fresh parsley
1 tablespoon chopped fresh coriander
$1/2$ teaspoon coconut essence
$3/4$ cup low-fat milk
$3/4$ cup low-salt fish stock
1 tablespoon reduced-salt soy sauce
$1/4$ teaspoon turmeric
freshly ground black pepper to taste
$1^{1}/2$ tablespoons cornflour
2 tablespoons water
4 green shallots, sliced
750g blue-eye cod (gemfish, kingfish, snapper or swordfish) cutlets or fillets, cut into 3cm pieces
300-400g snow peas (optional)

Heat oil in a saucepan. Add onion, ginger, garlic, chilli and capsicum. Cook for 3 minutes. Add parsley, coriander, coconut essence, milk, stock, soy sauce, turmeric and pepper. Bring to the boil. Reduce heat. Simmer for 5 minutes. Blend cornflour with water. Add cornflour mixture, shallots and fish to pan. Cook, stirring, until mixture boils and thickens. Reduce heat. Simmer for 8-10 minutes or until fish is cooked. Add snow peas (if using), in the last 3 minutes of cooking. Serve with steamed jasmine rice and stir-fried vegetables. *Recipe inspired by the Sydney Fish Marketing Authority*

WARM BALSAMIC FISH SALAD

Serves 6 as a light meal   **4g fat per serve**

2 teaspoons olive oil
500g blue-eye cod (Spanish mackerel, tuna, ocean trout, salmon, swordfish or mahi mahi) fillets, cut into 3cm cubes
8 fresh asparagus spears (or green beans), halved
200g (about 4 cups) mixed lettuce leaves
12 cherry tomatoes, quartered
1 Lebanese cucumber, sliced

BALSAMIC DRESSING
$1/3$ cup balsamic vinegar
2 tablespoons lemon (or lime) juice
2 teaspoons wholegrain mustard
freshly ground black pepper to taste

Heat oil in a non-stick frying or grill pan. Add fish. Cook over high heat until brown on both sides and flesh just flakes when tested. Boil or steam asparagus until just tender. Rinse under cold water. Drain well. Arrange lettuce, tomatoes, cucumber and asparagus in a serving bowl. Top with hot fish. Drizzle with dressing. Serve with crusty bread.
Dressing: Combine all ingredients in a screwtop jar. Shake well.

BAKED SNAPPER

Serves 4   **4.5g fat per serve**

2 (about 500g each) whole snapper (whole bream or trevally), fins trimmed
1 teaspoon olive oil
$1/2$ cup dry white wine
juice of 2 lemons
2 tablespoons chopped mixed fresh herbs (e.g. basil, oregano, thyme and coriander)
1 tablespoon chopped fresh parsley
2 cloves garlic, crushed (or to taste)
freshly ground black pepper to taste

Cut 3 diagonal slits in each side of the fish. Place in a flameproof baking dish. Combine oil, wine, lemon juice and mixed herbs in a saucepan. Bring to the boil. Boil for 3 minutes. Combine parsley, garlic and pepper. Spoon into cavity of each fish. Pour over wine mixture. Cover with foil. Bake at 180-190°C for 20 minutes or until just cooked. Alternatively, barbecue for 5 minutes each side or until just cooked. Remove fish from the baking dish. Keep warm. Place baking dish with cooking liquid on stove top. Bring to the boil. Reduce heat. Simmer, uncovered, until sauce is thick and glossy. To serve, spoon sauce over fish and accompany with rice and a mixed garden salad.

Barbecued Mullet

Serves 4   **10g fat per serve**

4 small whole mullet
2 teaspoons olive oil
juice of 1 lemon
2 teaspoons fresh thyme
freshly ground black pepper to taste
1 lemon, sliced
1 small Spanish (red) onion, sliced

Place each fish on a sheet of lightly greased foil. Combine oil and lemon juice. Brush over fish. Sprinkle with thyme and pepper. Arrange, alternate lemon and onion slices in cavity of fish. Wrap in foil. Barbecue, bake or grill until cooked. Serve with lemon wedges, a crisp green salad and crusty bread.

Barbecued Spicy Gemfish

Serves 4   **4g fat per serve**

1 cup reduced-salt vegetable (or tomato) juice
1 tablespoon reduced-salt soy sauce
1 clove garlic, crushed (optional)
1 teaspoon grated fresh ginger
$1/2$ teaspoon ground cumin
$1/4$ teaspoon chilli powder
500g gemfish (trevally, mullet, blackfish, barramundi or warehou) fillets, skin and bones removed, cut into serving size pieces
3 teaspoons cornflour

Combine vegetable juice, soy sauce, garlic (if using), ginger, cumin and chilli powder in a bowl. Add fish. Turn to coat. Cover. Marinate in the refrigerator for 1 hour. Drain. Reserve marinade. Barbecue or grill fish for 3 minutes each side or until cooked. Baste with reserved marinade during cooking. Combine reserved marinade and cornflour in a saucepan. Cook, stirring over low heat until mixture boils and thickens. To serve, spoon sauce over fish and accompany with grilled vegetables or a mixed lettuce salad. *Recipe courtesy of the Sydney Fish Marketing Authority*

Cook's tip: No-added-salt tomato puree diluted with wine or lemon juice can be used in place of vegetable juice.

Barramundi in Lime and Sparkling Wine

Serves 4   **6g fat per serve**

2 teaspoons olive oil
500 barramundi (flake, gemfish, ling or John dory) fillets
$1/2$ cup dry sparkling white wine
$1/4$ cup lime juice
freshly ground black pepper to taste
chopped fresh chives (optional)

Heat oil in a non-stick frying pan. Add fish. Cook until brown on one side. Turn fish over. Pour over wine and lime juice and sprinkle with pepper. Cover. Simmer for 5 minutes or until fish is cooked. Remove from pan. Keep warm. Bring liquid in pan to the boil. Season with pepper. Stir in chives (if using). Reduce heat. Simmer, uncovered, for 10 minutes or until liquid is reduced to a glaze. To serve, spoon glaze over fish and accompany with crusty bread and a radicchio or mixed lettuce salad.

Paprika Perch

Serves 4   **6g fat per serve**

dash Tabasco sauce
$1/2$ teaspoon paprika
juice of 1 lemon
2 teaspoons olive oil
500g sea perch (ling, ocean perch, gemfish or mirror dory) fillets

Combine Tabasco sauce, paprika, lemon juice and oil in a bowl. Add fish. Turn to coat. Cover. Marinate in the refrigerator for 1 hour. Drain. Reserve marinade.
Barbecue or grill fish for 2-3 minutes each side or until cooked. Baste with reserved marinade during cooking. Serve with pasta, grilled vegetables and Yoghurt Cucumber Sauce (pg 136).

Seared Tuna with Parsnip Puree

Serves 4   **16g fat per serve**

2 parsnips, peeled, chopped
2 potatoes, peeled, chopped
2 tablespoons low-fat natural yoghurt (or
    buttermilk)
freshly ground black pepper to taste
2 teaspoons olive (or vegetable) oil
4 (about 500g) tuna steaks

HERB SAUCE
1 cup chopped fresh parsley
3/4 cup fresh basil
1/3 cup fresh dill
1/4 cup white wine vinegar
1 tablespoon drained capers
2 tablespoons olive oil
1 clove garlic, crushed

Boil parsnips and potatoes until tender. Drain well. Mash parsnips, potatoes, yoghurt and pepper in a bowl. Heat a heavy-based non-stick frying pan or griddle pan until very hot. Add oil and tuna. Sear tuna for 1-2 minutes each side or until cooked as desired. The fish should flake, but still be pink in the centre.

To serve, spoon parsnip puree onto plates. Top with fish and drizzle with a spoonful of sauce or a splash of balsamic vinegar.

Sauce: Place all ingredients in a food processor. Process to combine.

Storage tip: Unused sauce will keep in a sealed jar in the refrigerator for up to 1 week.

Author's note: This recipe was inspired by chef Anthony Shaw from Canberra.

When buying fish fillets, look for shiny firm fillets with no discolouration and a pleasant sea smell. Whole fish should also have a pleasant sea smell with a bright lustrous skin and eyes that are bright and bulging, not sunken. The flesh should be firm and when touched spring back.

Top: Fish Poached in Wine (pg 42), Potato
Wedges (pg 95), Paprika Perch
Bottom: Barbecued Mullet, Barramundi in Lime
and Sparkling Wine, Barbecued Spicy Gemfish

Tomato Fish Casserole

Serves 4   **6.5g fat per serve**

4 (about 500g) firm white fish fillets
(e.g. gemfish, sea perch, snapper or
trevally), skin and bones removed
juice ½ lemon
freshly ground black pepper to taste
2 teaspoons olive oil
2 onions, sliced
1 tablespoon no-added-salt tomato paste
½ red capsicum, sliced
½ green capsicum, sliced
½ cup dry white wine
3 ripe tomatoes, sliced
⅓ cup chopped fresh parsley
2 teaspoons grated Parmesan cheese
2 teaspoon fresh breadcrumbs (preferably
made from 1-2 day old bread)

Place fish in a high-sided casserole dish. Pour over lemon juice. Sprinkle with pepper. Heat oil in a non-stick frying pan. Add onions. Cook until soft. Add tomato paste. Cook for 1-2 minutes. Add capsicums, wine, tomatoes and parsley. Simmer for 5-10 minutes or until capsicums are just soft. Arrange vegetables over fish. Combine Parmesan cheese and breadcrumbs. Sprinkle over vegetables. Bake at 190°C for 15 minutes or until fish is cooked. Serve with crusty bread and a garden salad.

F&P: If the fish has not been previously frozen this casserole can be frozen for up to 1 month.

Take care not to overcook fish as overcooking causes it to become tough and dry. It should be cooked until the flesh just flakes when pressed with a fork. Some fresh fish such as salmon, trout and tuna do not require as much cooking and many people like to simply sear the outside leaving the centre still pink.

Marinara Parcel

Serves 6   **6.5g fat per serve**

1 tablespoon olive oil
1 clove garlic, crushed
8 small mussels, removed from shells
350g firm fish fillets (e.g. tuna, blue-eye cod,
salmon or Spanish mackerel), skin and
bones removed, flesh chopped
1 cup dry white wine
¼ cup low-salt fish stock
3 tomatoes, chopped
2 spring onions, chopped
⅓ cup chopped fresh basil
2 tablespoons chopped fresh parsley
freshly ground black pepper to taste
12 scallops
300g spaghetti

Heat oil in a large non-stick frying pan. Add garlic. Cook for 1 minute. Stir in mussels and fish. Cook for 2 minutes. Add wine and stock. Cook for 2-3 minutes. Stir in tomatoes, onions, basil, parsley and pepper. Cook for 4-5 minutes or until fish is almost cooked. Remove from heat. Add scallops.
Cook spaghetti in boiling water for half the recommended time. Drain well. Add to seafood mixture. Toss. Place a large sheet of baking paper on a baking tray. Spoon seafood mixture into centre. Fold paper to make a parcel. Seal well so steam cannot escape during cooking. Bake at 220°C for 8-10 minutes.
To serve, open parcel at table and toss with a fork. Accompany with crusty Italian bread and a green salad.

Cook's tip: Rather than making one large parcel you may like to make individual parcels. The cooking time will be a little less than for one large parcel.

Tomato Fish Casserole, Redfish Rolls (pg 40), Marinara Parcel

POULTRY

TURKEY TROPICANA

Serves 4   **4g fat per sreve**

400g chopped cooked skinless turkey (or chicken)
1 small paw paw (mango, peaches or apricots),
    sliced
1 green capsicum, sliced
3/4 cup unsweetened orange juice
2 tablespoons lemon juice
2 tablespoons honey
2-4 teaspoons finely chopped fresh ginger
1 tablespoon cornflour
sesame seeds

Layer turkey, paw paw and capsicum in an
oiled shallow ovenproof dish. Combine next
5 ingredients in a saucepan. Cook, stirring,
until mixture boils and thickens. Pour over
the turkey. Bake at 180°C for 15 minutes or
until heated. To serve, sprinkle with sesame
seeds and accompany with steamed baby
potatoes and a green salad.

SESAME HONEY CHICKEN

Serves 4   **10g fat per serve**

2 tablespoons honey
1 teaspoon grated fresh ginger
1 teaspoon ground ginger
1 teaspoon reduced-salt soy sauce
1 teaspoon Worcestershire sauce
500g skinless chicken tenderloins (or thigh
    fillets)
2 tablespoons sesame seeds

Combine first 5 ingredients in a saucepan.
Bring to the boil. Remove from heat. Brush
over chicken. Sprinkle with sesame seeds.
Barbecue or grill chicken over moderate
heat for 4-5 minutes each side, brushing with
honey mixture. Alternatively, place chicken
in a baking dish. Cover. Bake at 180°C for
20-30 minutes or until cooked. Serve with
steamed rice and steamed or stir-fried
vegetables.

INDONESIAN GRILLED CHICKEN

Serves 4   **10g fat per serve**

3 green shallots, finely chopped
2 cloves garlic, crushed
1 teaspoon grated fresh ginger
1 teaspoon ground black pepper
1/2 teaspoon cumin seed
1/2 teaspoon turmeric
1 tablespoon lemon juice
4 (500g) chicken marylands, skin and fat removed
3/4 cup desiccated coconut
2 cups boiling water
1 sprig fresh basil

Combine shallots, garlic, ginger, pepper,
cumin, turmeric and lemon juice in a shallow
dish. Add chicken. Turn to coat. Cover.
Marinate in the refrigerator for at least
1 hour or overnight.
Place coconut in a bowl. Pour over water.
Stand for 30 minutes. Pour into a sieve lined
with muslin or a clean tea towel placed over
a bowl. Squeeze coconut to extract as much
liquid as possible. Reserve liquid and
1 tablespoon of coconut. Discard remaining
coconut. Drain chicken. Place reserved
liquid and coconut, basil and chicken in a
saucepan. Bring to the boil. Reduce heat.
Cover. Simmer for 10-15 minutes or until
chicken is just tender. Drain and reserve
cooking liquid. Cook chicken on a hot
barbecue or under a hot grill until well
browned. Brush occasionally with reserved
cooking liquid. Heat leftover cooking liquid
in a saucepan. To serve, spoon over chicken
and accompany with steamed or boiled rice
and steamed vegetables.

**Coconut, coconut milk and copha are high in
saturated fat. To replace coconut milk, add a
few drops of coconut essence to evaporated
skim milk or use the method described in the
recipe above.**

Chicken Pot Pie (pg 52), Turkey Tropicana,
Chicken and Mushroom Casserole (pg 52)

Chicken Pot Pie

Serve 6   **9g fat per serve**

2 teaspoons olive oil
125g button mushrooms, sliced
1 onion, chopped
1 carrot, chopped
1 stick celery, chopped
1 potato, finely chopped
2 tablespoons plain flour
1 1/2 cups low-salt chicken stock
1/4 cup chopped fresh parsley
1 teaspoon chopped fresh thyme (or
    1/2 teaspoon dried thyme)
freshly ground black pepper to taste
500g boneless, skinless cooked chicken meat,
    chopped
1/2 cup shelled fresh (or frozen) peas
1/3 cup sweet corn kernels
1/2 quantity Ricotta Pastry (pg 138)
low-fat milk

Heat oil in a non-stick frying pan. Add next 5 ingredients. Cook until tender. Add flour. Cook, stirring for 4-5 minutes, do not allow to brown. Add stock, herbs and pepper. Bring to the boil. Reduce heat. Simmer, uncovered, for 10 minutes, stirring occasionally. Cool. Stir in chicken, peas and corn. Spoon into a lightly greased 23cm casserole dish. Roll out pastry to cover dish. Place over dish. Trim edges. Brush with milk. Bake at 190°C for 30 minutes or until pastry is golden. Serve with steamed vegtables.

Warm Chicken Salad

Serves 6 as a light meal   **5g fat per serve**

1 tablespoon lime juice
1 teaspoon Worcestershire sauce
freshly ground black pepper to taste
3 (about 500g) skinless chicken breasts
1 small mango, chopped (reserve
    2 tablespoons for dressing)
1/2 red capsicum, sliced
1/3 cup green grapes
1 radicchio (cos or butter lettuce), leaves separated
2 tablespoons chopped roasted hazelnuts
2 tablespoons raisins

TROPICAL DRESSING

1/3 cup low-fat natural yoghurt
2 tablespoons reserved mango flesh (see
    above), mashed
1 teaspoon Dijon mustard
2 teaspoons red wine vinegar
1 teaspoon chopped fresh parsley
1 teaspoon chopped fresh mint
freshly ground black pepper to taste

Place first 3 ingredients in a bowl. Add chicken. Toss to coat. Drain. Cook under a hot grill for 5-7 minutes each side or until just cooked. Cool slightly. Cut into slices. Place chicken, mango, capsicum and grapes in a bowl. Drizzle with dressing. Toss. To serve, spoon salad onto lettuce leaves and sprinkle with hazelnuts and raisins.
Dressing: Whisk together all ingredients.

Chicken and Mushroom Casserole (Microwave)

Serves 4   **3.5g fat per serve**

500g skinless chicken pieces, trimmed of
    visible fat
250g button mushrooms
1 green capsicum, sliced
4 spring onions, halved
1 tablespoon cornflour
1/2 cup low-salt chicken stock
1/2 cup low-fat milk
freshly ground black pepper to taste
1/4 cup chopped fresh parsley

Preheat a large browning dish on HIGH (100%) for 5 minutes. Add chicken. Cover with kitchen paper. Cook on HIGH (100%) for 10 minutes turning over after 5 minutes. Remove. Drain on kitchen paper. Add mushrooms, capsicum and onions. Cook for 3 minutes. Blend cornflour with a little of the stock. Stir in remaining stock and milk. Stir into dish. Season with pepper. Return chicken to dish. Stir well. Cover. Cook for 20 minutes or until chicken is cooked. Stir once during cooking. To serve, sprinkle with parsley and accompany with rice or noodles.

Warm Chicken Salad; Orange-glazed Chicken,
Chicken and Paw Paw Kebabs (recipes pg 56)

CHICKEN RATATOUILLE

Serves 4   **8.5g fat per serve**

1 tablespoon olive oil
500g skinless chicken breast fillets, cut into
    3cm pieces
2 large zucchini, sliced
1 small eggplant, chopped
1 medium onion, thinly sliced
1/2 red capsicum, chopped
1/2 green capsicum, chopped
250g mushrooms, sliced
425g canned no-added-salt tomatoes, undrained
1/4 cup dry white wine
1 clove garlic, crushed
11/2 teaspoons dried basil
1 tablespoon chopped fresh parsley
1 stick celery, sliced
freshly ground black pepper to taste

Heat oil in a large high-sided non-stick frying pan. Add chicken. Cook for 3 minutes or until lightly browned. Add next 5 ingredients. Cook for 15 minutes, stirring occasionally. Stir in remaining ingredients. Cook for 5 minutes or until chicken is tender. Serve with boiled fettuccine or rice.

LEMON CHICKEN AND ALMONDS

Serves 6   **10g fat per serve**

juice of 1 lemon
1 teaspoon brown sugar
2 teaspoons reduced-salt soy sauce
2 tablespoons dry sherry
4 (about 500g) skinless chicken thigh (or
    breast) fillets, thinly sliced
1 tablespoon peanut (or vegetable) oil
1 onion, chopped
1 teaspoon grated fresh ginger
1 large red capsicum, sliced
300g broccoli (or beans), chopped
1/3 cup almonds (or cashews), toasted
2 teaspoons cornflour
2 tablespoons water (or vegetable) stock

Combine first 5 ingredients in a bowl. Toss. Cover. Marinate in the refrigerator for at least 30 minutes. Drain. Reserve marinade. Heat half the oil in a wok. Stir-fry chicken in batches until cooked. Set aside. Heat remaining oil in wok. Add onion and ginger. Stir-fry for 1 minute. Add capsicum, broccoli and almonds. Stir-fry for 1 minute. Combine cornflour, water and reseved marinade. Return chicken to wok. Add cornflour mixture. Stir-fry for 1 minute or until mixture boils. Serve with steamed or boiled rice.

ROLLED CHICKEN BREAST WITH PECAN RICE SEASONING

Serves 4   **9g fat per serve**

4 large boneless, skinless chicken breast fillets
1 cup undrained, chopped canned no-added-
    salt tomatoes
2 tablespoons chopped fresh basil
1/2 cup dry white wine
1 teaspoon dried oregano
freshly ground black pepper to taste

PECAN RICE SEASONING

1/2 cup cooked rice
1/4 cup chopped fresh parsley
2 tablespoons chopped pecans
1/2 Spanish (red) onion, finely chopped
6 dried apricots, finely chopped
1 tablespoon low-fat natural yoghurt
1 teaspoon lemon juice

Pound chicken fillets to flatten. Place one-quarter of the seasoning on one end of each chicken fillet. Roll up. Secure with wooden toothpicks. Place in an oiled casserole dish. Combine remaining ingredients. Pour over chicken. Cover with foil. Bake at 180°C for 20 minutes. Uncover. Bake for 10 minutes or until chicken is cooked. Serve with a green salad or steamed vegtables.
Seasoning: Combine all ingredients in a bowl.

Soy (even reduced-salt), fish, oyster, hoisin, plum and many other flavour enhancing sauces are high in salt and should be used sparingly to enhance flavour not to overpower food. Try ginger, garlic, shallots, herbs and spices to add flavour without salt.

Coq au Vin (pg 56), Chicken Ratatouille,
Rolled Chicken Breast with Pecan Rice Seasoning

CHICKEN AND PAW PAW KEBABS

Serves 6 **17g fat per serve**

juice of 2 lemons
1 clove garlic, chopped
2 teaspoons chopped fresh ginger
2 tablespoons peanut oil
4 single skinless chicken breast fillets, cut into
    large pieces
1 slightly underripe paw paw, chopped
1 green shallot, chopped
1/3 cup no-added-salt peanut butter
freshly ground black pepper to taste
1/3 cup low-fat natural yoghurt
1 tablespoon chilli sauce

Combine the juice of 1 lemon, half the garlic, ginger and oil in a bowl. Add chicken. Toss to coat. Cover. Marinate in the refrigerator for at least 1 hour or overnight.
Thread chicken and paw paw onto skewers. Heat remaining oil in a non-stick frying pan. Add remaining garlic, ginger and lemon juice, shallot, peanut butter and pepper. Cook, stirring until heated. As the sauce thickens add a little water. Stir in yoghurt and chilli sauce. Heat, do not allow to boil. Barbecue or grill kebabs. To serve, spoon sauce over kebabs and accompany with steamed or boiled rice and snow pea sprouts.

TANDOORI CHICKEN

Serves 6 **5g fat per serve**

1.3kg whole chicken, skin and fat removed
150g low-fat natural yoghurt
1 teaspoon grated fresh ginger
1 clove garlic, crushed
1/4 teaspoon chilli powder
1/2 teaspoon paprika
1/2 teaspoon ground cumin
1 teaspoon turmeric
1/2 teaspoon garam masala
pinch saffron powder (or saffron colouring)

Make four shallow cuts in each chicken breast. Combine remaining ingredients. Reserve 2 tablespoons of yoghurt mixture. Rub remaining yoghurt mixture over chicken (the best way to thoroughly coat the chicken

is to rub the mixture in using your hands). Cover. Marinate in the refrigerator for at least 2 hours. Bake at 180°C for 30 minutes. Drain any fat from pan. Spread reserved yoghurt mixture over chicken. Bake for 30-60 minutes or until cooked. Serve with lemon wedges, boiled basmati rice, steamed vegetables and microwaved pappadams.

ORANGE-GLAZED CHICKEN

Serves 4 **11g fat per serve**

2 teaspoons olive oil
4 large skinless chicken breast fillets
300g baby carrots
1 tablespoon grated fresh ginger
1 tablespoon brown sugar (or honey)
3/4 cup fresh orange juice
freshly ground black pepper to taste
400g sugar snap peas (snow peas or other
    vegetables of your choice)
2 tablespoons slivered almonds, toasted

Heat oil in a non-stick frying pan. Add chicken. Cook until brown on both sides. Set aside. Add carrots and ginger. Cook for 2-3 minutes. Return chicken to pan. Stir sugar, orange juice and pepper into pan. Simmer for 8-10 minutes or until chicken is cooked. Add peas. Cook for 3 minutes. To serve, sprinkle with almonds and accompany with steamed vegetables.

COQ AU VIN

Serves 6 **8g fat per serve**

1/3 cup plain flour
1 teaspoon paprika
10 skinless chicken drumsticks
1 tablespoon olive oil
1 clove garlic, crushed
10 raw pickling onions, peeled
2 rashers lean bacon, trimmed of visible fat,
    chopped
250g button mushrooms
2 1/2 cups low-salt chicken stock
2 cups dry red wine
1/3 cup brandy
bouquet garni
1 tablespoon chopped fresh parsley

Combine flour and paprika in a plastic bag. Add chicken. Shake to coat. Heat oil in a flameproof casserole dish. Add chicken, garlic, onions, bacon and mushrooms. Cook until lightly browned. Add stock and wine. Cook, stirring, until sauce boils and thickens. Stir in brandy and bouquet garni. Cover. Bake at 180°C for 45 minutes or until chicken is cooked. To serve, remove bouquet garni, sprinkle with parsley and accompany with steamed green vegetables.

CHICKEN AND NOODLE STIR-FRY

Serves 4   **6.5g fat per serve**

500g hokkien noodles
2 (250g) skinless chicken breast fillets, cut into thin slices
2 teaspoons cornflour
1 tablespoon reduced-salt soy sauce
1 teaspoon sugar
1 tablespoon vegetable oil
2 cloves garlic, crushed
4 green shallots, cut into 5cm pieces
1 tablespoon oyster sauce
$1/4$ cup water
250g mung bean sprouts
$1/2$ red capsicum, thinly sliced
extra shallot greens, thinly sliced for garnish

Place noodles in a bowl. Cover with boiling water and loosen with a fork. Drain.
Combine chicken, 1 teaspoon cornflour, 1 teaspoon soy sauce, sugar and 2 teaspoons oil in a bowl. Cover. Stand for 10 minutes.
Heat remaining oil in a wok. Add garlic. Stir-fry until golden. Add shallots pieces and chicken. Stir-fry for 2 minutes. Add noodles, remaining soy sauce and oyster sauce. Blend remaining cornflour with water. Add to pan. Stir-fry for 5 minutes or until chicken is just cooked. Add bean sprouts. Stir-fry until heated. To serve, place in serving bowls and scatter with capsicum and extra shallots.
Recipe inspired by Hounn Ngov

Top: Sesame Honey Chicken (pg 50), Chicken and Noodle Stir-fry, Lemon Chicken and Almonds (pg 54)
Bottom: Tandoori Chicken,
Indonesian Grilled Chicken (pg 50)

MEAT

CHILLI BEAN PIE WITH COUNTRY CORN CRUST

Serves 8   **8g fat per serve**

2 teaspoons olive oil
1 onion, chopped
1 small fresh red chilli, finely chopped
1 clove garlic, crushed
$1/4$ cup no-added-salt tomato paste
$1/2$ teaspoon chilli powder
500g lean beef mince
1 large tomato, chopped
$2/3$ cup low-salt chicken stock (or dry red wine)
420g canned red kidney (or pinto) beans, rinsed and drained
$1/2$ cup grated carrot
$1/2$ cup grated zucchini
few drops Tabasco sauce

COUNTRY CORN CRUST

1 cup polenta
$3/4$ cup self-raising flour
1 cup buttermilk (or low-fat milk)
1 egg

Heat oil in a non-stick frying pan. Add onion, chilli and garlic. Cook until onion is soft. Add tomato paste and chilli powder. Cook for 1 minute. Add mince. Cook for 2-3 minutes or until mince changes colour. Add tomato, stock and beans. Simmer for 8-10 minutes or until mixture thickens. Add carrot and zucchini. Season with Tabasco sauce. Spoon mixture into greased ovenproof dish. Place large spoonfuls of corn crust mixture on top. Bake at 190°C for 25-30 minutes or until crust is golden. Serve with a green salad and low-fat natural yoghurt.

Corn Crust: Combine dry ingredients in a bowl. In a separate bowl, whisk together buttermilk and egg. Stir into dry ingredients. Mix until just combined. Do not overmix.

SHEPHERD'S PIE

Serves 6   **8g fat per serve**

2 teaspoons vegetable oil
1 onion, chopped
500g lean cooked roast lamb (or beef), trimmed of visible fat and sinew, finely chopped
2 tablespoons plain flour
$1/2$ teaspoon dry mustard
1 cup low-salt chicken stock (or water)
1 teaspoon Worcestershire sauce
2 tablespoons chopped fresh parsley
1 teaspoon grated lemon rind
1 carrot, thinly sliced
$1/2$ cup celery, chopped
freshly ground black pepper to taste
4 large potatoes
$1/4$ cup low-fat milk
1 tablespoon chopped fresh chives
$1/4$ cup grated reduced-fat mozzarella cheese (optional)

Heat oil in a large saucepan. Add onion and meat. Cook until onion is soft. Stir in flour and mustard. Gradually stir in stock, Worcestershire sauce, parsley, lemon rind, carrot, celery and pepper. Cook, stirring until mixture boils and thickens. Boil potatoes until tender. Mash with milk and chives. Spoon meat mixture into a lightly greased ovenproof dish. Top with mashed potato and if desired, rough surface with a fork to give an attractive rustic appearance. Sprinkle with mozzarella cheese (if using). Bake at 180°C for 20-30 minutes or until lightly browned. Serve with a green salad.

To extend meals, especially casseroles and soups and to add variety and fibre, add beans or legumes to the mixture. Try kidney beans in casseroles, chick peas in salads, and split peas or lentils in soups.

Chilli Bean Pie with Country Corn Crust, Shepherd's Pie, Hungarian Goulash (pg 60)

Hungarian Goulash

Serves 6   **5.5g fat per serve**

2 teaspoons light olive oil
2 onions, chopped
2 cloves garlic, crushed
$1/2$ teaspoon freshly ground black pepper
1 teaspoon caraway seeds
1 tablespoon paprika
600g beef topside, trimmed of visible fat, cut
     into 5cm pieces
$1/2$ cup no-added-salt tomato paste
3 cups low-salt beef stock
2 large potatoes, chopped
2 green capsicums, chopped
7 tomatoes, peeled, seeded, chopped

Heat oil in a heavy-based saucepan. Add onions, garlic, pepper, caraway seeds and paprika. Cook until onions are soft. Add beef. Cook until brown on all sides. Stir in tomato paste. Cook for 1-2 minutes. Add stock. Bring to the boil. Reduce heat. Cover. Simmer for $1^1/2$ hours. Add potatoes and capsicums. Cover. Simmer for 30 minutes or until potatoes are tender. Stir in tomatoes. Cook until just heated through. Serve with boiled rice or pasta and a garden salad.

F&P: Can be frozen for up to 1 month.

Glazed Meatloaf

Makes 14 thick slices   **5.5g fat per slice**

500g lean beef mince
$1^1/2$ cups fresh breadcrumbs (preferably made
     from 1-2 day old bread)
$1/2$ cup grated pumpkin
$1/2$ cup grated zucchini
$1/4$ cup chopped fresh parsley
2 tablespoons grated Parmesan cheese
2 eggs, lightly beaten
freshly ground black pepper to taste
$1/2$ cup dry red wine
2 tablespoons no-added-salt tomato paste
1 tablespoon olive oil
$1/2$ cup hot water
1 clove garlic, crushed
$1/2$ teaspoon sugar

Combine mince, breadcrumbs, pumpkin, zucchini, parsley, cheese, eggs, pepper and half the wine in a bowl. Press mixture into a greased and lined 13 x 21cm loaf pan. Bake at 170°C for 10 minutes. Combine remaining wine, tomato paste, oil, water, garlic and sugar. Pour over meatloaf. Bake for 40 minutes longer or until cooked.

To serve, cut meatloaf in thick slices, spoon over any sauce that acculumates during cooking and accompany with steamed vegetables. Also delicious served cold with crusty bread and a crisp garden salad.

Beef and Vegetable Stir-fry

Serves 6   **9g fat per serve**

2 tablespoons dry red wine
1 tablespoon reduced-salt soy sauce
$1/2$ teaspoon sesame oil
$1^1/2$ teaspoons grated fresh ginger
500g lean beef rump (or sirloin), cut into
     5cm strips
2 tablespoons peanut oil
2 onions, cut into 8 wedges
125g mushrooms, sliced
2 sticks celery, sliced
250g green beans, halved
6 snow peas
1 large carrot, cut into strips
230g canned water chestnuts, drained

Combine wine, soy sauce, sesame oil and ginger in a bowl. Add beef. Cover. Marinate in the refrigerator for at least 1 hour.

Heat 1 tablespoon peanut oil in a wok. Add onions and mushrooms. Stir-fry for 3 minutes. Add celery. Stir-fry for 1 minute. Add remaining vegetables. Stir-fry for 2 minutes or until beans are tender. Remove vegetables. Heat remaining oil in wok. Add meat. Stir-fry until just cooked. Return vegetables to wok. Stir-fry to reheat. Serve with steamed rice.

PORK VINDALOO

Serves 6   **5.5g fat per serve**

750g diced lean pork
4 large onions, finely chopped
4 cloves garlic, crushed
1¹/₂ tablespoons garam masala
2 teaspoons chopped fresh chilli
1 teaspoon freshly ground black pepper
1 cup brown vinegar
1 tablespoon brown sugar
1 tablespoon vegetable oil

Combine pork, onions, garlic, garam masala, chilli, pepper, vinegar and sugar in a bowl. Cover. Marinate in the refrigerator for at least 1 hour or overnight. Drain. Reserve marinade. Heat oil in a large heavy-based saucepan. Add pork mixture. Cook, stirring over high heat until pork changes colour. Add reserved marinade. Bring to the boil. Reduce heat. Cover. Simmer for 1 hour. Remove cover. Simmer for 30 minutes or until pork is tender. Serve with steamed basmati rice and vegetables.

F&P: Can be frozen for up to 3 months.

BEEF CASSEROLE WITH CARAMELISED VEGETABLES

Serves 4   **9.5g fat per serve**

500g diced lean beef
2 tablespoons cornflour
1 tablespoon olive oil
¹/₂ cup dry red wine
¹/₂ cup low-salt beef stock (or water)
¹/₂ cup undrained, chopped canned no-added-
     salt tomatoes
1 large carrot, chopped
1 large parsnip, chopped
2 onions, cut into wedges
1 tablespoon brown sugar
¹/₃ cup chopped fresh parsley

Toss beef in cornflour. Heat half the oil in a heavy-based, non-stick saucepan. Add beef. Cook, stirring, until brown on all sides. Add

Beef and Vegetable Stir-fry, Glazed Meatloaf, Beef Casserole with Caramelised Vegetables

wine, stock and tomatoes. Bring to the boil. Reduce heat. Cover. Simmer for 1-1¹/₂ hours or until meat is tender.
Boil or steam carrot and parsnip until nearly cooked. Just before serving, heat remaining oil in a non-stick frying pan. Add onions. Cook until soft. Stir in sugar. Cook until sugar melts. Add carrot and parsnip. Toss. Cook over low heat for 4-5 minutes or until vegetables are tender and well coated with mixture. To serve, top beef with caramelised vegetables, sprinkle with parsley and accompany with steamed rice.

Premium lean mince is more expensive than regular mince, however it contains very little fat and therefore does not shrink as much during cooking.

Japanese Barbecue Veal

Serves 4 **3g fat per serve**

4 (500g) veal fillet steaks, trimmed of visible fat

TERIYAKI MARINADE

2 teaspoons reduced-salt soy sauce
$^1/_4$ cup rice wine (or dry sherry)
1 teaspoon brown sugar
1 teaspoon finely grated fresh ginger
2 teaspoons teriyaki sauce
1 clove garlic, crushed

Combine veal and marinade in a bowl. Cover. Marinate in the refrigerator for at least 1 hour. Drain. Reserve marinade.
Barbecue or grill veal until brown on both sides and cooked as desired. Brush with marinade during cooking. Serve with steamed rice and vegetables.
Marinade: Combine all ingredients.

Barbecued Mustard Steak

Serves 4 **7.5g fat per serve**

1 tablespoon hot English mustard
1 tablespoon honey
1 clove garlic, crushed
1 teaspoon grated fresh ginger
$^1/_2$ cup beer
cracked black peppercorns to taste
4 (500g) beef sirloin steaks, trimmed of
    visible fat

Combine mustard, honey, garlic, ginger, beer and peppercorns in a bowl. Add steaks. Cover. Marinate in the refrigerator for at least 1 hour or overnight.
Drain steaks. Reserve marinade. Barbecue or grill until cooked as desired. Brush with reserved marinade during cooking. Serve with grilled vegetables or salad and hot crusty bread.

To add interest and flavour to grilled lean meat and poultry baste with mustards, chutneys, beer, wine and herbs during cooking.
Marinating and then basting with the marinade during cooking also helps keep lean meat moist and tender.

Apricot and Pork Kebabs

Serves 4 **4g fat per serve**

500g diced lean pork
16 small dried apricots

APRICOT MARINADE

$^1/_4$ cup chilli sauce
1 teaspoon peanut oil
1 tablespoon strained apricot jam
1 teaspoon hoisin sauce
1 tablespoon cider vinegar
1 teaspoon sambal oelek
$^1/_2$ teaspoon dry mustard
2 cloves garlic, crushed

Combine pork and marinade in a bowl. Cover. Marinate in the refrigerator for at least 1 hour. Drain. Reserve marinade.
Place apricots in a bowl. Cover with hot water. Stand for 1 hour. Drain.
Thread pork and apricots, alternately, onto skewers. Barbecue or grill kebabs until cooked. Brush with marinade during cooking.
Marinade: Combine all ingredients.

Cajun Lamb Kebabs

Serves 4 **4.5g fat per serve**

$^1/_2$ teaspoon cracked black peppercorns
$^1/_2$ teaspoon ground oregano
$^1/_2$ teaspoon ground chillies
1 teaspoon paprika
1 teaspoon ground cumin
1 teaspoon brown sugar
500g diced lean lamb (fillets, round or topside
    steak)
1 red capsicum, cut into cubes
1 green capsicum, cut into cubes
1 Spanish onion (red), cut into wedges

Combine peppercorns, oregano, chillies, paprika, cumin and sugar in a plastic bag. Add lamb. Shake to coat. Set aside for 30 minutes. Thread lamb and vegetables, alternately, onto skewers. Barbecue or grill kebabs until cooked as desired. Serve with lemon wedges or bottled apricot chutney, bread and a green salad.

Japanese Barbecue Veal, Apricot and Pork Kebabs,
Grilled Vegetables (pg 136), Cajun Lamb Kebabs,
Barbecued Mustard Steak

Irish Stew with Dumplings

Serves 6   **8.5g fat per serve**

500g diced lean lamb
$1/4$ cup plain flour
2 tablespoons chopped fresh parsley
1kg potatoes, thinly sliced
2 onions, sliced
4 carrots, sliced
2 sticks celery, sliced
mixed fresh herbs
freshly ground black pepper to taste
1 cup low-salt chicken (or beef) stock
1 cup low-fat milk

PARSLEY DUMPLINGS

$1/2$ cup wholemeal self-raising flour
$1/2$ cup white self-raising flour
1 tablespoon canola (or sunflower) oil
1 egg, lightly beaten
1 tablespoon chopped fresh parsley
1 tablespoon low-fat milk

Combine lamb, flour and parsley in a plastic bag. Toss to coat. Layer potatoes, lamb, onions, carrots, celery, herbs and pepper in a flameproof casserole dish. Finish with a layer of potatoes. Pour over stock and milk. Bring to the boil over a medium heat. Reduce heat. Cover. Simmer for $1^3/4$ hours. Top with dumplings. Cover. Cook for 20 minutes or until lamb is tender.
Dumplings: Sift flours into a bowl. Add oil, egg, parsley and milk. Mix to make a firm dough. Roll pieces of dough into 2.5cm balls.

Steak Diane

Serves 4   **9g fat per serve**

4 (500g) lean beef rib eye (or scotch fillet)
    steaks, trimmed of visible fat
freshly ground black pepper to taste
3 teaspoons light olive oil
1 clove garlic, crushed
2 green shallots, finely chopped
2 tablespoons brandy
2 tablespoons Worcestershire sauce
$1/2$ cup chopped fresh parsley
$1/2$ cup evaporated skim milk

Pound meat until about 1cm thick. Sprinkle with pepper. Heat 2 teaspoons of oil in a non-stick frying pan. Add steaks. Cook until brown on both sides. Drain on kitchen paper. Heat remaining oil in pan. Add garlic and shallots. Cook for 2 minutes. Stir in brandy, Worcestershire sauce, and half the parsley. Cook for 1 minute. Stir in milk. Cook for 2 minutes. Return beef and remaining parsley to pan. Cook until tender. Serve with steamed potatoes, beans and grilled tomatoes.

Beef Stroganoff

Serves 4   **8.5g fat per serve**

$1/2$ cup plain flour
1 tablespoon sweet paprika
500g lean beef rump steak, trimmed of visible
    fat, cut into thin strips
1 tablespoon olive oil
1 onion, sliced
425g canned no-added-salt tomatoes,
    undrained
200g button mushrooms, sliced
$1/4$ teaspoon ground nutmeg
$1/2$ teaspoon dried basil
1 tablespoon finely chopped fresh parsley
1 tablespoon Worcestershire sauce
250g low-fat natural yoghurt

Combine flour, paprika and beef in a plastic bag. Toss to coat. Shake off excess flour. Heat oil in large non-stick frying pan. Add onion. Cook until soft. Cook beef in batches for 5 minutes or until brown. Return beef to pan. Add tomatoes, mushrooms, nutmeg, basil, parsley and Worcestershire sauce. Bring to the boil. Reduce heat. Cover. Simmer for 10 minutes or until tender. Just before serving, stir in yoghurt. Heat through. Do not allow to boil. Serve with macaroni and steamed vegetables.

Low-fat yoghurt can replace sour cream in many recipes, however take care that you do not allow the mixture to boil or it will curdle. For thick and creamy yoghurt, drain the yoghurt before using (see tip on pg 108).

Irish Stew with Dumplings, Beef Stroganoff, Steak Diane

THAI-STYLE STIR-FRIED LAMB

Serves 6　　　　　　　　**9g fat per serve**

1 tablespoon vegetable oil
500g lamb fillets, trimmed of visible fat, cut
　　into 5cm strips
2 tablespoons very thinly sliced fresh ginger
2 small fresh red chillies, chopped
root and stems of 1 coriander plant, finely sliced
250g broccoli, chopped
200g snow peas (or beans)
1 red capsicum, cut in thin strips
4 green shallots, cut in 5 cm lengths
1/3 cup evaporated skim milk
1/4 teaspoon coconut essence
1 teaspoon fish sauce
1/4 cup dry roasted cashews (or peanuts, optional)

Heat oil in a wok. Cook lamb in batches over high heat until brown. Return to wok. Add ginger, chillies and coriander. Stir-fry for 1 minute. Add broccoli, snow peas, capsicum and shallots. Stir-fry for 2 minutes or until vegetables are just tender. Combine milk, coconut essence and fish sauce. Stir into pan. Cook, stirring, until heated. Just before serving, stir in cashews (if using). Serve with steamed jasmine rice.

MIDDLE EASTERN LAMB

Serves 6 as a light meal　　**9g fat per serve**

600g lean lamb mince
1/4 cup chopped fresh parsley
1 tablespoon chopped fresh mint
2 tablespoons chopped fresh coriander
2 tablespoons lemon juice
1 onion, finely chopped
1/2 teaspoon ground allspice
1 teaspoon ground cumin
cracked black peppercorns to taste
olive oil
2 tablespoons pine nuts

Process first 9 ingredients in a food processor to combine. Refrigerate for 30 minutes. Press evenly over base of a lightly greased 23cm square slab cake pan. Brush with oil. Score meat mixture into 4-5cm squares. Press a pine nut in the centre of each square. Cook

under a hot grill for 15-20 minutes or until cooked. Alternatively, bake at 180°C for 10-15 minutes. Serve with Tabbouleh (pg 97) and Pide (Turkish Flat Bread pg 126).

FRUITY LAMB CURRY WITH BANANA RAITA

Serves 6　　　　　　　　**11g fat per serve**

1 cup desiccated coconut
3 cups low-fat milk
1 tablespoon vegetable oil
500g diced lean lamb
1 large onion, sliced
1 tablespoon mild curry powder
2 tablespoons plain flour
2 tablespoons fruit chutney
1 red apple, cored and chopped
1/4 cup sultanas
425g canned pineapple pieces in natural juice,
　　drained
1/4 cup dry roasted cashews

BANANA RAITA

1 cup low-fat natural yoghurt
2 bananas, thinly sliced
1 small fresh green chilli, thinly sliced
1 teaspoon lemon juice

Place coconut and milk in a saucepan. Slowly bring to the boil. Remove from heat. Stand 10 minutes. Strain. Reserve 2 tablespoons of coconut. Discard remaining coconut.
Heat oil in a large saucepan. Add lamb and onion. Cook until brown. Sprinkle over curry powder. Cook for 2 minutes. Push lamb to one side of pan. Stir flour into pan juices. Gradually stir in milk. Add chutney, apple, sultanas and pineapple. Cover. Simmer for 20 minutes or until tender. Sprinkle with nuts. Serve with raita, steamed rice, reserved drained coconut and chopped cucumber.
Curry recipe courtesy of Dairy Farmers
Banana Raita: Combine all ingredients in a bowl. Cover. Refrigerate.

F&P: Curry can be frozen, without cashews, for up to 1 month.

Thai-style Stir-fried Lamb, Middle Eastern Lamb, Fruity Lamb Curry with Banana Raita, Lamb in Lemon Sauce (pg 72)

CREAMY SHREDDED VEAL

Serves 4   **4g fat per serve**

500g veal leg steaks, trimmed of visible fat,
    cut into thin strips
2 teaspoons olive oil
2 green shallots, sliced
1 rasher lean bacon, trimmed of visible fat,
    finely chopped
1 cup sliced mushrooms
1 tablespoon cornflour
1 cup low-fat milk
1/2 cup dry white wine
freshly ground black pepper to taste
1/2 teaspoon dried oregano
1 tablespoon chopped fresh chives

Heat oil in a non-stick frying pan. Add veal. Cook until tender. Set aside. Add shallots and bacon. Cook until shallots are soft. Add mushrooms. Cook until soft. Blend cornflour with milk. Stir in wine, pepper, oregano and cornflour mixture. Cook, stirring, until sauce boils and thickens slightly. Return veal to pan. Reduce heat. Simmer for 2-3 minutes or until heated. Just before serving, stir in chives. Serve with boiled noodles and steamed spinach.

Cook's tip: Chicken breast can also be used in this recipe.

VEAL VIVANT

Serves 4   **8g fat per serve**

1 tablespoon olive oil
4 (500g) lean veal steak medallions (or fillets)
1 cup orange juice
juice of 1 lemon
1 teaspoon reduced-salt soy sauce
1/4 cup dry white wine
1/4 cup low-salt chicken stock
freshly ground black pepper to taste
12 asparagus spears (or green beans)

Heat oil in a non-stick frying pan. Add veal. Cook for 1-2 minutes each side. Remove. Add orange and lemon juices, soy sauce, wine, stock and pepper. Bring to the boil. Reduce heat. Simmer for 10-15 minutes or until mixture starts to thicken. Add veal. Cook for 5 minutes. Stir in asparagus. Cook for 5 minutes or until veal is tender and well coated with sauce. To serve, top veal with asparagus, spoon over sauce and accompany with steamed rice and vegetables. *Recipe courtesy Peter Wallace, CEO Heart Foundation*

VEAL CASSEROLE

Serves 4   **3g fat per serve**

1 teaspoon canola margarine
4 (500g) veal chops, trimmed of visible fat
1 onion, sliced
125g button mushrooms, quartered
2 carrots, sliced
2 sticks celery, sliced
1 zucchini, sliced
1 red capsicum, seeded and chopped
425g canned no-added-salt tomatoes, undrained
1 cup low-salt chicken stock
1/2 cup dry white wine
1 tablespoon no-added-salt tomato paste
2 tablespoons chopped fresh basil
freshly ground black pepper to taste
1 tablespoon cornflour blended with
    1/4 cup water

Melt margarine in a heavy-based saucepan. Add veal. Cook until brown on both sides. Set aside. Add onion. Cook until soft. Add mushrooms, carrots, celery, zucchini and capsicum. Cook for 1 minute. Stir in tomatoes, stock, wine, tomato paste, basil and pepper. Bring to the boil. Reduce heat. Return veal to pan. Cover. Simmer for 35-40 minutes or until tender. Stir cornflour mixture into pan. Cook, stirring, until mixture boils and thickens. Serve with steamed rice or crusty bread. *Recipe courtesy Gold'n Canola*

F&P: Can be frozen for up to 3 months.

If time allows, prepare meat casseroles ahead of time, chill and any fat will set on the surface. This can be easily removed before reheating. When making casseroles it is worth making a double quantity so that you can freeze half to have on hand for a quick meal.

Osso Bucco

Serves 6   **1g fat per serve**

750g veal shanks, trimmed of visible fat
2 carrots, chopped
2 onions, chopped
2 sticks celery, chopped
1 clove garlic, crushed
2 teaspoons grated lemon rind
1 bay leaf
$1/2$ teaspoon dried thyme
freshly ground black pepper to taste
425g canned no-added-salt tomatoes, undrained
$1/2$ cup dry white wine
$1/4$ cup chopped fresh parsley

Cook veal in a non-stick saucepan until brown all over. Set aside. Add carrots, onions, celery and garlic. Cook for 3-4 minutes. Stir in remaining ingredients, expect parsley. Return veal to pan. Bring to boil. Reduce heat. Cover. Simmer for $1^1/2$ hours or until tender, stirring occasionally. Discard bay leaf. Sprinkle with parsley and serve with steamed rice and green vegetables.

F&P: Can be frozen for up to 1 month.
Cook's tips: Ask the butcher to saw the veal shanks into 5cm pieces. Lean diced beef can be used instead of the veal shanks.

Home-style Roast Lamb

Serves 6   **7.5g fat per serve**

1kg lean leg of lamb, trimmed of visible fat
2 tablespoons bottled mint jelly
2 tablespoons lemon juice
1 tablespoon olive oil
2 tablespoons chopped fresh parsley
1 clove garlic, crushed
6 potatoes, halved
6 pieces sweet potato
6 large pieces pumpkin
2 cups peas (or beans)
6 baby carrots
1 tablespoon cornflour
1 cup low-salt chicken stock

Place lamb on a wire rack in a baking dish. Pour enough water into dish to come one-third of the way up the sides. Combine jelly, lemon juice, oil, parsley and garlic. Spread over lamb. Bake at 180°C for $1^1/2$ hours or until cooked. Brush occasionally with pan juices during cooking. Arrange potatoes, sweet potatoes and pumpkin on rack beside lamb or in a separate baking dish. Place in oven about 40 minutes before lamb is cooked. Boil or steam peas and carrots. Place lamb on serving platter. Cover with foil. Rest for 10-15 minutes before carving. Discard water and fat from pan. Blend cornflour with stock. Pour into pan. Cook, stirring, until mixture boils and thickens. To serve, carve lamb in to thin slices and accompany with vegetables and gravy.

Spinach and Ricotta Veal Rolls

Serves 4 as a main meal   **15g fat per serve**
Serves 8 as a light meal   **7.5g fat per serve**

4 large spinach (or silverbeet) leaves
8 (500g) very thin lean veal leg steaks (or schnitzels)
$1^1/4$ cups (250g) ricotta (or cottage) cheese
1 tablespoon chopped fresh parsley
1 teaspoon dried oregano
1 teaspoon freshly ground black pepper
1 tablespoon olive oil
$1/2$ cup dry red wine
$1/2$ cup no-added-salt tomato puree

Blanch spinach. Drain well. Place half a spinach leaf on each piece of veal. Spread with ricotta cheese. Sprinkle with parsley, oregano and pepper. Roll up. Secure with string. Heat oil in a non-stick frying pan. Add rolls. Cook until brown on all sides. Add wine and tomato puree. Cover. Simmer for 30 minutes or until cooked as desired. Serve with boiled noodles tossed with chopped parsley and a salad or steamed vegetables.

Venison with Port Glaze and Macadamias

Serves 4   **15g fat per serve**

4 (500g) lean venison fillet steaks, trimmed of
  visible fat
1 tablespoon vegetable oil
1/3 cup raw macadamia nuts
2 tablespoons cranberry sauce
1/3 cup port

CRANBERRY MARINADE

1 carrot, finely chopped
1 onion, finely chopped
2 cups red wine vinegar
1 tablespoon whole black peppercorns
1/4 cup cranberry sauce

Combine venison and marinade in a bowl.
Cover. Marinate in the refrigerator for at least
1 hour or overnight. Drain. Discard marinade.
Heat oil in non-stick frying pan. Add venison.
Cook over high heat until brown all over. Set
aside. Drain fat from pan. Add nuts. Cook
until golden. Drain on kitchen paper. Stir
cranberry sauce and port into pan. Return
venison to pan. Cover. Simmer for 10 minutes
or until cooked as desired. Remove venison
from pan. Keep warm. Bring sauce to the
boil. Reduce heat. Simmer until reduced to a
shiny glaze. To serve, slice venison and
arrange on serving plates. Sprinkle with nuts
and pour over glaze. Accompany with
steamed mixed vegetables.
Marinade: Combine all ingredients.

Lamb in Lemon Sauce

Serves 4   **6.5g fat per serve**

1 tablespoon virgin olive oil
4 lamb shortloin (backstrap or fillet), trimmed of
  visible fat and sinew
grated rind and juice of 3 lemons

Heat oil in a non-stick frying pan or griddle
pan. Add lamb. Cook over high heat until
brown on all sides and cooked as desired.
Pour over lemon rind and juice. Cook for
2 minutes. Remove lamb from pan. Cover
with foil. Stand for 5 minutes. To serve, slice

lamb and place on a bed of salad greens.
Spoon over sauce from pan and accompany
with boiled pasta or rice. *Recipe courtesy
Penny Farrell*

Cook's tip: The juice and grated rind of
lemons, limes, oranges and grapefruit as
well as flavoured vinegars give a refreshing
lively flavour to meat dishes and replace the
need for salt.

Peppered Kangaroo with Beetroot Vinaigrette

Serves 4   **10g fat per serve**

500g boneless kangaroo rump (or loin),
  trimmed of visible fat
cracked black peppercorns
2 teaspoons olive oil

BEETROOT VINAIGRETTE

2 (about 225g) fresh beetroot
1/4 cup cider vinegar
1 tablespoon olive oil
1/3 cup low-salt chicken stock
1 tablespoon chopped fresh dill
1 teaspoon ground black pepper
1 teaspoon sugar

Roll meat in peppercorns. Heat a non-stick
frying pan. Add oil. When hot, add meat.
Cook over high heat until brown all over.
Transfer to a baking dish. Bake at 180°C for
20-30 minutes or until cooked as desired. To
serve, cool slightly and cut into slices. Serve
with Beetroot Vinaigrette, damper or rolls
and a green salad or steamed vegetables.
Beetroot Vinaigrette: Boil or steam
beetroot. Cool. Grate or chop. Puree with
remaining ingredients.

**Kangaroo, venison, camel, buffalo and emu
are becoming more readily available and, in
general, tend to be very lean. It is important
not to overcook game meats or they will be
dry and tough. Modern farming techniques
means that it is possible to grill, roast and
barbecue many of the cuts. It is often helpful
to marinate game to add moisture and
complement the bold flavours.**

Venison with Port Glaze and Macadamias,
Peppered Kangaroo with Beetroot Vinaigrette

Spicy Pork Chops

Serves 4   **9g fat per serve**

2 tablespoons crunchy no-added-salt
    peanut butter
1 teaspoon sesame seeds
1 teaspoon mild curry powder
1/2 teaspoon ground coriander
1/4 teaspoon chilli powder
1 clove garlic, crushed
4 (500g) pork loin chops, trimmed of visible fat
freshly ground pepper to taste

Combine first 6 ingredients in a bowl. Season chops with pepper. Brush one side of each chop with some peanut butter mixture. Cook under a hot grill for 2-3 minutes. Turn chops. Brush with remaining peanut butter mixture. Cook for 3-4 minutes or until brown and cooked. Serve with grilled mushrooms, a salad and crusty bread.

Stir-fried Pork and Rice Noodles

Serves 4   **5.5g fat per serve**

400g lean pork fillet, trimmed of visible fat, cut
    into bite-sized pieces
1 tablespoon reduced-salt soy sauce
1 teaspoon grated fresh ginger
150g rice noodles
3 teaspoons vegetable oil
1 small white onion, cut into wedges
1 red capsicum, chopped
1 cup cauliflower florets
1 cup broccoli florets (or 12 snow peas)
2 tablespoons water
1/2 teaspoon chilli sauce

Combine pork, soy sauce and ginger in a bowl. Cook noodles in boiling water. Drain well. Heat 2 teaspoons oil in a wok. Add pork. Stir-fry until tender. Set aside. Heat remaining oil in wok. Add onion, capsicum, cauliflower and broccoli. Stir-fry for 2 minutes. Add water. Cover. Cook for 2 minutes or until cauliflower is just tender. Return pork to wok. Add noodles and chilli sauce. Toss. Cook, stirring until heated.

Pork in Prune Sauce

Serves 4   **12g fat per serve**

2 teaspoons olive oil
4 (500g) pork loin medallions, trimmed of
    visible fat
1 onion, finely chopped
1 clove garlic, crushed
1 teaspoon French mustard
1 teaspoon paprika
1/3 cup chopped pitted prunes
1 tablespoon port
2 teaspoons cornflour
3/4 cup low-fat milk
1/2 cup water
1/3 cup slivered almonds, toasted
2 green shallots, green part only, finely sliced

Heat oil in a non-stick frying pan. Add pork. Cook until brown. Set aside. Add onion and garlic. Cook for 5 minutes. Add mustard, paprika, prunes and port. Cook for 2 minutes. Combine cornflour, milk and water. Stir into pan. Cook, stirring, until mixture boils and thickens slightly. Return pork to pan. Simmer for 10 minutes or until cooked. Serve sprinkled with almonds and shallots. Accompany with boiled rice and steamed vegetables.

Pork with Apple Cider Sauce

Serves 4   **3g fat per serve**

1 teaspoon olive oil
1 onion, sliced
2 green apples, peeled, cored, cut into wedges
1 cup apple cider
1 tablespoon chopped pitted prunes
1 tablespoon lemon juice
2 (500g) lean pork fillets, trimmed of visible fat

Heat oil in non-stick frying pan. Add onion and apples. Cook for 5 minutes. Add cider and prunes. Bring to boil. Reduce heat. Simmer for 5 minutes. Stir in lemon juice. Place pork fillets in a lightly greased, shallow ovenproof dish. Pour over apple mixture. Cover. Bake at 180°C for 30 minutes or until pork is just cooked. To serve, slice pork and accompany with boiled or steamed rice and steamed vegetables.

FRUITY PORK PARCELS

Serves 4   **7g fat per serve**

4 (500g) pork leg steaks (or schnitzels),
    trimmed of visible fat
$^1/_3$ cup fruit chutney
2 tablespoons packaged breadcrumbs
1 green shallot, thinly sliced
$^1/_2$ fresh mango (peach or banana), peeled,
    sliced
1 tablespoon canola oil
2 teaspoons cornflour
$^3/_4$ cup chicken stock
2 teaspoons no-added-salt tomato paste
1 tablespoon reduced-salt soy sauce

Pound steaks until very thin. Combine
chutney, breadcrumbs and shallot. Spread
over steaks. Place a slice of fruit at one end
of each steak. Roll up. Secure with string.
Heat oil in a non-stick frying pan. Add rolls.
Cook over medium heat until brown all over.
Combine cornflour, stock, tomato paste and
soy sauce. Stir into pan. Cook, stirring, until
sauce boils and thickens slightly. Cover.
Reduce heat. Simmer for 35 minutes or until
tender. Remove string before serving.
Accompany with boiled noodles and
steamed vegetables.

**Stir-frying is a great low-fat cooking method.
For quick and even cooking keep stir-fries
moving during cooking and cut food in even-
sized pieces. Cut meat thinly across the grain,
mix with a little oil (2 teaspoons oil per 500g
meat) and stir-fry in batches in a hot wok or
frying pan with garlic and ginger or other
flavourings of your choice.**

Top: Pork with Apple Cider Sauce, Fruity Pork
Parcels, Stir-fried Pork and Rice Noodles
Bottom: Pork Vindaloo (pg 61), Spicy
Pork Chops, Pork in Prune Sauce

MEAT COOKING CHART

Use this chart to help you select the most suitable cut of meat for your chosen cooking method. These methods are recommended by the Australian Meat and Livestock Corporation (AMLC) and the Australian Pork Corporation for cooking National Heart Foundation approved cuts. The Heart Foundation also recommends that all meat is trimmed of visible fat before cooking.

COOKING METHOD	MEAT AND CUT
Stir-fry	**Beef:** lean beef strips, rump steak, sirloin steak, fillet steak, boneless blade steak, round steak, topside steak **Lamb:** lean lamb strips, round steak, topside steak, eye of loin, fillet **Pork:** diced lean pork, lean leg strips
Barbecue and pan-fry	**Beef:** rump steak, sirloin steak, fillet steak, eye of round steak, blade steak **Lamb:** 'Frenched' cutlets, round steak, topside steak, eye of loin, fillet **Pork:** loin chop, loin steak, loin cutlet, diced pork (as kebabs), rump steak, leg steak, topside steak, silverside For best results always preheat the grill or pan. Brush meat with oil, rather than putting the oil in the pan. Add meat and cook until desired doneness is reached. Do not turn meat too often and remember the more cooked these cuts are the tougher they become. If you like your meat well-done move it to a cooler part of the pan, grill or barbecue, after the intital searing, to complete the cooking.
Grill	**Beef:** When grilled (i.e. cooked under an element) very lean beef can become tough and dry because there is no direct heat to seal in the juices. If you wish to grill lean beef the AMLC recommends making kebabs and marinating them prior to cooking, this helps retain the moisture in the meat. **Lamb:** 'Frenched' cutlets, round steak, topside steak, eye of loin, fillet **Pork:** loin chop, midloin butter steak, loin steak, loin cutlet, rump steak, leg steak, fillet, loin steak, leg schnitzel. Take care not to overcook pork when grilling or it will become tough and dry.
Casserole/stew	**Beef:** diced round steak, diced blade steak, well-trimmed chuck steak and shin beef **Lamb:** lean diced lamb from the leg, round steak, topside steak, diced forequarter (well-trimmed), well-trimmed lamb shanks (available from progressive butchers and supermarkets fully trimmed as 'drumsticks') **Pork:** diced pork For best results, cut meat into even-sized pieces. Dry and sear in small batches, over a high heat in a deep-sided pan until meat is just brown. Return all meat to pan or place in a casserole. Add vegetables, flavourings and liquid. Cook over low heat or in a low oven until tender. The tougher the cut of meat the more slowly it should be cooked.
Roast/bake	**Beef:** fillet steak, sirloin steak, rump steak, blade steak, topside steak **Lamb:** topside mini roast, round mini roast, rack of lamb, trimmed traditional leg and shoulder roasts, well trimmed Easy Carve leg and shoulder roasts, well trimmed lamb shanks and 'drumsticks' **Pork:** loin steak, loin (rind removed before cooking), fillet, leg schnitzel, topside, silverside

Home-style Roast Lamb (pg 70), Stuffed Jacket Potatoes (pg 94),
Roasted Corn on the Cob (pg 86)

PASTA, PIZZA & RICE

BEEF AND SPINACH LASAGNE

Serves 8   **16g fat per serve**

2 teaspoons olive oil
1 large onion, chopped
1 clove garlic, crushed
1 red capsicum, chopped
500g lean beef mince
810g canned no-added-salt tomatoes,
    undrained and chopped
2 tablespoons no-added-salt tomato paste
1 carrot, sliced
100g mushrooms, sliced
2 zucchini, sliced
2 tablespoons finely chopped fresh basil
12 sheets instant lasagne
250g packet frozen spinach, thawed and
    drained on kitchen paper
1 cup (200g) ricotta cheese
250g reduced-fat mozzarella cheese, grated

Heat oil in a non-stick frying pan. Add onion and garlic. Cook until soft. Add capsicum and mince. Cook until mince is browned, breaking up any large pieces. Drain off fat. Stir in tomatoes, tomato paste, carrot, mushrooms, zucchini and basil. Bring to the boil. Reduce heat. Simmer for 20 minutes or until thickened.

Line a deep rectangular ovenproof dish with one-third of the lasagne sheets Spoon over half the meat mixture. Top with half the spinach and one-third of the ricotta and mozzarella cheeses. Repeat with remaining ingredients, ending with a layer of lasagne sheets. Sprinkle with remaining cheese. Bake at 180°C for 40 minutes. Stand for 10 minutes. Serve with green salad and bread.

F&P: Can be frozen for up to 2 months.

If you cannot find lean mince, cook ordinary mince in a little olive or canola oil, drain off any fat, then chill. The fat will set and can be removed or rinsed off before proceeding with the recipe. Cook extra and freeze to use for burgers, pastries or as a quick pasta sauce.

PENNE, CHEESE AND TOMATO BAKE

Serves 6   **4.5g fat per serve**

300g penne (or macaroni) pasta
425g canned no-added-salt tomatoes,
    undrained, chopped
2 spring onions, chopped
2 tablespoons chopped fresh basil
1 teaspoon dried oregano
1 tablespoon grated Parmesan cheese
$3/4$ cup grated reduced-fat mozzarella cheese
$1/2$ cup fresh breadcrumbs (preferably made
    from 1-2 day old bread)
freshly ground black pepper to taste

Partially cook pasta. Drain well. Combine pasta, tomatoes, onions, basil, oregano and half the Parmesan cheese in a bowl. Spoon half into an oiled deep casserole dish. Sprinkle with $1/2$ cup of mozzarella cheese, the remaining Parmesan cheese, half the breadcrumbs and pepper. Spoon over remaining pasta mixture. Sprinkle with remaining mozzarella cheese and breadcrumbs. Bake at 220°C for 20 minutes or until pasta is cooked. Serve with a garden salad.

Variation: For variety, vegetables such as grated zucchini and chopped mushrooms can be added to the pasta mixture. For something more substantial add drained, canned tuna or cooked, chopped skinless chicken.

Do not throw out stale bread. Grate or process to make breadcrumbs for toppings, stuffings or use in other recipes requiring fresh breadcrumbs. For crisper breadcrumbs bake in a slow oven until dry. Cool and store in an airtight container.

Paella (pg 84), Beef and Spinach Lasagne,
Penne, Cheese and Tomato Bake

Pasta Sauces

Pasta is a great low-fat food and is available in many shapes, colours and flavours. For a complete meal serve with a green salad and crusty bread. Experiment with sauces to suit your taste using tomato bases, ricotta cheese and pureed vegetables instead of cream and cheese sauces. Sauces should complement not smother the pasta.

Broccoli and Pine Nut Sauce

Serves 2 as a main	**18g fat per serve**
Serves 4 as an entree	**9g fat per serve**

170g broccoli, chopped
1/4 cup low-salt chicken stock
1/2 small onion, chopped
1 small clove garlic, crushed
1 tablespoon olive oil
2 tablespoons white wine vinegar
1 tablespoon grated Parmesan cheese
1 teaspoon chopped fresh basil
2 tablespoon pine nuts

Combine broccoli, stock and onion in a saucepan. Bring to boil. Simmer for 5 minutes or until just soft. Cool slightly. Place in a food processor. Add garlic, oil, vinegar, Parmesan cheese and basil. Process to combine. To serve, stir sauce through hot cooked pasta and sprinkle with pine nuts.

Pork, Mushroom and Lemon Sauce

Serves 6   **9.5g fat per serve**

1 1/2 tablespoons olive oil
500g lean pork rump steak, trimmed of visible fat, cut into thin slices (or minced)
225g button mushrooms, sliced
1 cup evaporated skim (or low-fat) milk
grated rind of 1 lemon
freshly ground black pepper to taste
2 tablespoons chopped fresh parsley
750g fettuccine, cooked
2 tablespoons grated Parmesan cheese

Heat half the oil in a non-stick frying pan. Add pork. Cook for 10 minutes. Add mushrooms. Cook for 5 minutes, stirring occasionally. Stir in milk, lemon rind and pepper. Bring to the boil. Reduce heat. Simmer, uncovered, for 3 minutes or until tender. Just before serving, stir in parsley.
To serve, spoon sauce over hot fettuccine. Toss. Sprinkle with Parmesan cheese and accompany with a tossed green salad or steamed vegetables.

Pasta with Chilli Chicken Sauce

Serves 6   **7.5g fat per serve**

1 tablespoon canola oil
1 red capsicum, chopped
1 onion, chopped
1 clove garlic, crushed
500g skinless chicken thigh (or breast) fillets, thinly sliced
425g canned no-added-salt tomatoes, undrained, chopped
1 cup dry white wine
1 tablespoon chilli sauce
1 teaspoon chopped fresh chilli
1 teaspoon dried basil
1/2 teaspoon dried oregano
freshly ground black pepper to taste
500g pasta of your choice, cooked
1/4 cup chopped fresh parsley

Heat oil in a non-stick frying pan. Add capsicum, onion and garlic. Cook until soft. Add chicken. Cook, stirring until tender. Stir in tomatoes, wine, chilli sauce, chilli, basil, oregano and pepper. Simmer for 15 minutes or until thickened, stirring occasionally.
To serve, spoon sauce over hot pasta. Toss. Sprinkle with parsley and serve with a salad and crusty bread. *Recipe courtesy of Gold'n Canola*

For a delicious rich flavour in dishes where fat has been removed add tomato paste to the sauteed onion and cook until it turns a rust colour before adding meat, vegetables, liquids or other ingredients. This is a great method to use for sauces, casseroles and soups.

ITALIAN MEAT SAUCE

Serves 6   **6.5g fat per serve**

2 teaspoons light olive oil
1 onion, chopped
1 clove garlic, crushed
1 stick celery, sliced
1 tablespoon no-added-salt tomato paste
300g lean beef mince
810g canned no-added-salt tomatoes, undrained
2 finger eggplants, thickly sliced (or 1 standard
    eggplant, chopped)
1 tablespoon chopped fresh basil
freshly ground black pepper to taste
500g spaghetti, cooked

Heat oil in a non-stick frying pan. Add onion, garlic and celery. Cook for 2 minutes. Add tomato paste. Cook for 2 minutes or until mixture changes colour. Add mince. Cook, stirring until mince browns. Add tomatoes, eggplants, basil and pepper. Reduce heat. Simmer, uncovered for 15 minutes or until mince is cooked, stirring occasionally.
To serve, spoon sauce over hot spaghetti and accompany with a salad.

F&P: Sauce can be frozen for up to 3 months.

SMOKED SALMON AND RICOTTA SAUCE

Serves 2 as a main   **9g fat per serve**
Serves 4 as an entree   **4.5g per serve**

100g smoked salmon, thinly sliced (or 210g
    canned no-added-salt salmon)
$1/2$ cup (100g) ricotta cheese
1 tablespoon lemon juice
cracked black pepper to taste
2 tablespoons chopped fresh basil (or dill)
1 teaspoon poppy seeds

Combine all ingredients in a bowl. Lightly fold through hot pasta.

Top: Italian Meat Sauce served over spaghetti, Rich Vegetable Sauce (pg 82), Broccoli and Pine Nut Sauce, Pork, Mushroom and Lemon Sauce, Fresh Tomato and Basil Sauce (pg 82), Pasta with Chilli Chicken Sauce
Bottom: Layered Pizza Pie (pg 83); Beef Pizza, Sardine and Grilled Capsicum Pizza, Classic Italian Pizza (recipes pg 84)

SARDINE SAUCE

Serves 4   **13g fat per serve**

1 tablespoon olive oil
1 onion, chopped
2 leeks, sliced
1 tablespoon no-added-salt tomato paste
1/2 cup dry white wine
1 cup undrained, chopped canned no-added-
    salt tomatoes
2 tablespoons lemon juice
2 tablespoons chopped fresh parsley
freshly ground black pepper
10-12 fresh sardines, filleted

Heat oil in a non-stick frying pan. Add onion and leeks. Cook until soft. Add tomato paste. Cook for 3 minutes. Stir in wine, tomatoes, lemon juice, parsley and pepper. Cook for 5 minutes. Add sardines. Cook over low heat for 5 minutes, stirring to break up sardines. To serve, spoon sauce over hot pasta. Toss.

Cook's tip: Ask the fishmonger to fillet the sardines or use canned reduced-salt sardines.

RICH VEGETABLE SAUCE

Serves 4   **2g fat per serve**

1 teaspoon olive oil
1 onion, chopped
1 clove garlic, crushed
1 rasher lean reduced-salt bacon, trimmed of
    visible fat, rinsed, patted dry on kitchen paper
1 yellow (red or green) capsicum, cut into
    thin strips
1 small zucchini, cut into thin strips
1 small carrot, cut into thin strips
1/3 cup dry white wine
1 cup chopped fresh (or canned) tomatoes
1 cup English spinach, shredded
freshly ground black pepper to taste

Heat oil in a non-stick frying pan. Add onion, garlic and bacon. Cook until onion is soft. Add capsicum, zucchini and carrot. Cook over medium heat for 2 minutes. Add wine, tomatoes, spinach and pepper. Cook for 5 minutes or until sauce thickens slightly. To serve, spoon over hot pasta. Toss.

Variations: Use this sauce as base for seafood sauces. Add tuna, scallops or mixed seafood with the vegetables.

TOMATO AND MUSHROOM SAUCE

Serves 4 as a main   **3g fat per serve**
Serves 6 as an entree   **2g fat per serve**

2 teaspoons olive oil
1 small onion, chopped
1 clove garlic, crushed
1 tablespoon chopped fresh basil
425g canned no-added-salt tomatoes,
    undrained
freshly ground black pepper to taste
400g mushrooms, sliced
1/2 teaspoon ground nutmeg
1 tablespoon chopped fresh parsley
grated Parmesan cheese (optional)
low-fat natural yoghurt (optional)

Heat half the oil in a non-stick frying pan. Add onion and garlic. Cook until soft. Add basil, tomatoes and pepper. Cook over low heat for 10-15 minutes or until thickened. In a separate pan, heat remaining oil. Add mushrooms. Cook until soft. Stir in nutmeg and parsley. To serve, spoon tomato sauce over hot pasta. Toss. Top with mushrooms. Serve with Parmesan cheese or yoghurt (if using).

FRESH TOMATO AND BASIL SAUCE

Serves 2 as a main   **5g fat per serve**
Serves 4 as an entree   **2.5g fat per serve**

4 firm Roma tomatoes, finely chopped
1 small clove garlic, crushed
10 basil leaves, shredded
freshly ground black pepper to taste
2 teaspoons virgin olive oil

Combine tomatoes, garlic, basil and pepper in a bowl. Drizzle with olive oil. Cover. Refrigerate for at least 30 minutes. To serve, spoon tomato mixture over hot cooked pasta. Toss. Accompany with a green salad.

Rice, Lentils and Cashews

Serves 4   **12g fat per serve**

1 cup brown lentils
1 tablespoon vegetable oil
2 small onions, chopped
1 teaspoon grated fresh ginger
1 cup long-grain rice
3 1/2 cups water
2 tablespoons chopped fresh coriander
1 teaspoon cumin seeds
50g dry roasted cashews

Place lentils in a bowl. Pour over cold water to cover. Cover. Stand overnight. Drain well. Heat oil in a non-stick frying pan. Add onions and ginger. Cook until soft. Stir in lentils and rice. Cook, stirring, for 2 minutes. Add water, coriander and cumin seeds. Bring to the boil. Reduce heat. Cover. Simmer for 15 minutes or until rice is cooked. Stand, covered, for 5 minutes. Stir in cashews. Serve with a salad or steamed vegetables.

Layered Pizza Pie

Serves 8   **1g fat per serve (crust only)**

2 sachets (14g) dry yeast
1 teaspoon sugar
1 1/2 cups warm water
1/4 cup warm low-fat milk
3 1/3 cups plain flour
fillings of your choice

Combine yeast, sugar and 1/2 cup of water in a bowl. Set aside in a warm place for 10 minutes or until frothy. Add remaining water and milk. Mix well. Sift flour into a large bowl. Make a well in the centre. Pour in yeast mixture. Knead until well combined. Knead on a lightly floured surface until smooth and elastic. Place in an oiled bowl. Turn to coat with oil. Cover. Stand in a warm place for 1 hour or until doubled in size. Punch down. Knead for 2 minutes or until smooth. Cut dough into 3 pieces. Shape each piece into a ball. Roll or press each ball into a 20cm circle, making one slightly larger than the others. Place filling on one of the smaller circles, leaving a 2cm border. Top with a second smaller circle of dough. Seal edges. Top with second layer of filling then the larger circle of dough. Seal edges well. Brush with a little milk or oil. Bake at 200°C for 30 minutes or until golden and the base sounds hollow when tapped.

Filling ideas: Here are two ideas for fillings for a Layered Pizza Pie. Do not be afraid to try your own combinations, just remember to choose low-fat ingredients for a healthy and delicious pie.

Vegetable and Chicken Layered Pie
1st layer: Grated pumpkin, zucchini and reduced-fat mozzarella cheese, chopped fresh parsley, roasted capsicum and pesto.
2nd layer: Sun-dried tomatoes, ricotta cheese, thinly sliced, cooked, skinless chicken breast, chopped fresh basil, grilled eggplant and chopped Spanish (red) onion.

Fish and Cheese Layered Pie
1st layer: Tomato paste, drained, canned tuna in springwater (or drained, canned no-added-salt salmon), chopped spring onion, and sliced mushrooms.
2nd layer: Sliced bocconcini, sliced tomato, chopped fresh basil and chopped Spanish (red) onion.

Short cut: The scone or damper dough (pg 122 or 126) can be used for the crust of this pie rather than this yeast dough.

Sun-dried tomatoes are very flavoursome and can add interest to all kinds of dishes. Look for the dried version rather than those packed in oil. To use the dried tomatoes, simply place in hot water and allow to rehydrate for 10 minutes. The tomatoes are now ready to use as required. The soaking liquid makes a tasty addition to soups, rice and casseroles.

Pizzas

Fresh and frozen pizza bases make quick and healthy meals. Read labels carefully as many of the frozen bases have unnecessary added fat. If you like making your own but do not have much time, try a scone or damper mixture. Pita bread also makes a great crisp base. Pizzas are as healthy as the topping you put on them, remember use cheese (even low- and reduced-fat) sparingly. Here are a few ideas to start you off.

Pizza Topping Ideas

Classic Italian: Alternate slices of fresh tomato, bocconcini and chopped fresh basil on pizza base. Sprinkle with freshly ground black pepper. Bake at 220°C for 12-15 minutes.

Barbecued Chicken: Top pizza base with slices of barbecued skinless chicken breast, Spanish (red) onion rings, chopped tomato, thyme and grated reduced-fat mozzarella cheese. Bake at 220°C for 10-12 minutes.

Seafood and Salad: Spread pizza base with pesto or top with chopped tomato. Top with chopped red capsicum and sliced smoked salmon (or drained, flaked canned no-added-salt salmon), mussels (or chopped fresh fish) and spoonfuls of ricotta cheese. Bake at 220°C for 12 minutes. To serve, pile a handful of lettuce leaves and a few halved cherry tomatoes in the centre of the pizza.

Tandoori Lamb: Spread pizza base with no-added-salt tomato paste. Bake at 220°C for 10 minutes. Coat lean lamb strips in tandoori sauce. Drain. Stir-fry for 1-2 minutes. Scatter over pizza base. Top with onion rings and combined low-fat natural yoghurt and mint. Sprinkle with grated reduced-fat mozzarella cheese. Bake at 220°C for 5-10 minutes.

Beef Pizza: Heat a little olive oil in a non-stick frying pan. Add lean beef strips. Stir-fry for 2-3 minutes or until brown. Drain on kitchen paper. Combine no-added-salt tomato paste with crushed garlic, dried oregano leaves and freshly ground black pepper. Spread over pizza base, leaving a 1.5cm border. Top with beef, sliced mushrooms and sliced green capsicum. Sprinkle with grated reduced-fat mozzarella cheese. Bake at 230°C for 20-25 minutes.

Sardine and Grilled Capsicum Pizza: Spread pizza base with no-added-salt tomato paste. Top with roasted red, green and yellow capsicums, cut into strips, sliced tomatoes, drained, canned reduced-salt sardines and sliced black olives. Sprinkle with grated reduced-fat mozzarella cheese. Season with freshly ground black pepper and shredded fresh oregano. Bake at 200°C for 10 minutes.

Paella

Serves 6   **7.5g fat per serve**

large pinch of saffron threads
2 tablespoons boiling water
1 tablespoon olive oil
2 skinless chicken breast fillets, chopped
l large onion, chopped
1 red capsicum, chopped
1 green capsicum, chopped
2 cloves garlic, crushed
1 1/2 cups long-grain rice
3 1/2 cups low-salt chicken stock, approximately
250g fish fillets, cut into large pieces (e.g. ling, gemfish, tuna or blue-eye cod)
8 uncooked medium prawns, shelled, leaving tails intact
12 small black mussels in shells
1 cup frozen peas

Combine saffron and boiling water. Stand for 5 minutes.
Heat oil in a non-stick frying pan. Add chicken. Cook until lightly browned. Add onion and capsicums. Cook for 2 minutes. Add garlic and rice. Cook for 2 minutes. Stir in saffron mixture and enough stock to cover rice by 1cm. Cover. Cook over very low heat for 15 minutes. Place fish, prawns, mussels and peas on top of rice. Cover. Cook for 5 minutes or until seafood is tender. Discard any unopened mussels. Serve with a large salad.

Spinach and Mushroom Pilau

Serves 8 as a side dish   **6g fat per serve**

1 tablespoon olive oil
1 onion, chopped
1 clove garlic, crushed
3 cups white long-grain rice
5 cups low-salt chicken stock (or water)
$^1/_2$ teaspoon cumin seeds
4 mushrooms, chopped
1 finger eggplant (or small zucchini), chopped
2 cups shredded fresh spinach (or 150g frozen
     spinach)
$^1/_2$ cup currants
1 teaspoon grated orange rind
$^1/_4$ cup slivered almonds, toasted

Heat oil in a saucepan. Add onion and garlic.
Cook for 1 minute. Add rice. Cook, stirring,
for 5 minutes. Stir in stock and cumin seeds.
Bring to the boil. Reduce heat. Cover with a
tight fitting lid. Simmer for 10 minutes. Add
mushrooms and eggplant. Cook for 5 minutes
or until rice is tender and liquid is absorbed.
Stir in spinach, currants and orange rind.
Cook for 5 minutes. To serve, sprinkle with
almonds.

Thai Chicken Fried Rice

Serves 6   **7g fat per serve**

2 cups jasmine (or long-grain) rice
1 tablespoon peanut oil
1 clove garlic, crushed
1 tablespoon grated fresh ginger
250g skinless chicken breast fillets, cut
     into strips
3 green shallots, chopped, keep green and
     white parts separate
125g bean shoots
$^1/_2$ red capsicum, thinly sliced
$^1/_4$ cup chopped fresh coriander
2 tablespoons fish sauce
2 teaspoons reduced-salt soy sauce
1 teaspoon chilli sauce
50g snow pea sprouts (optional)
$^1/_4$ cup roasted cashews (or almonds)

Rice, Lentils and Cashews (pg 83), Spinach and
Mushroom Pilau, Thai Chicken Fried Rice

Boil or steam rice until just tender.
Heat oil in a wok. Add garlic and ginger. Stir-
fry for 2 minutes. Add chicken and white
part of shallots. Stir-fry until chicken
changes colour. Add bean shoots, capsicum,
coriander and chopped green part of
shallots. Stir-fry for 1-2 minutes. Add rice,
fish sauce, soy sauce and chilli sauce. Stir-fry
over high heat until heated. Serve immediately
with snow pea sprouts (if using) and cashews.

**Leftover pasta makes a great salad base or
can be used to extend soups and casseroles.
For a quick and easy bake mix leftover pasta
with tomatoes, vegetables, fish or skinless
chicken and a little stock or wine. Place in an
ovenproof dish, sprinkle with reduced-fat
mozzarella cheese and bake until heated
through and the top is golden and crisp.**

SALADS & VEGETABLES

SPANISH BEEF SALAD

Serves 8   **5.5g fat per serve**

6 (600g) lean beef round (or topside) steaks,
    trimmed of visisble fat
4 cups (200g) mixed salad leaves
8 baby new potatoes, boiled
100g snow peas, blanched
2 carrots, cut into thin strips, blanched
1 large Spanish (red) onion, sliced
1 tablespoon olive oil
1 tablespoon lemon juice
2 tablespoons balsamic vinegar
1 clove garlic, crushed
$1/2$ teaspoon dried oregano
freshly ground black pepper to taste
1 tablespoon Parmesan cheese shavings

Barbecue or grill steaks until just pink in the
centre or until cooked as desired.
Combine salad leaves, potatoes, snow peas,
carrots and onion in a serving bowl. Place
oil, lemon juice, vinegar, garlic, oregano and
pepper in a jar. Shake to combine. Spoon
over salad. Toss. Cut steaks into slices.
Arrange over salad. Scatter with Parmesan
cheese.

ROASTED CORN ON THE COB

Serves 4   **2g fat per serve**

4 fresh corn on the cob, husks intact
2 tablespoons chopped mixed fresh herbs
    (e.g. basil, marjoram, tarragon, chervil,
    chives, coriander, oregano)
freshly ground black pepper to taste

Loosen husks from corn taking care not to
detach from cob. Remove silk. Rinse
carefully under cold water. Drain well.
Sprinkle corn with herbs and pepper. Pull
husks back over cob. Tie in place with string.
Dampen husks with a little water. Place on a
baking tray. Bake at 190°C, or cook on the
barbecue, for 10-15 minutes or until tender.

ORIENTAL PORK SALAD

Serves 4   **2.5g fat per serve**

$1/4$ cup dry sherry
1 tablespoon reduced-salt soy sauce
1 tablespoon hoisin sauce
2 cloves garlic, crushed
300g lean pork fillet
1 mignonette lettuce, leaves separated
$1/4$ red cabbage, shredded
1 large carrot, cut into thin strips
$1/2$ white radish, cut into thin strips
juice of 2 limes
$1/2$ teaspoon sesame oil

Combine sherry, soy sauce, hoisin sauce and
garlic in a bowl. Add pork. Cover. Marinate
in the refrigerator for at least 2 hours or
overnight. Drain pork. Place in baking dish.
Bake at 200°C for 15 minutes. Cool.
To serve, arrange lettuce, cabbage, carrot
and radish on individual serving plates. Cut
pork into thin slices. Arrange attractively on
top of salad. Place lime juice and sesame oil
in a jar. Shake to combine. Drizzle over salad.
Serve with crusty bread.

Cook's tip: Sesame oil has an intense
flavour and is great in marinades or as a
seasoning for stir-fries and rice. Only a few
drops are required to give a distinctive
flavour to a dish.

**To reduce the amount of oil in a classic oil and
vinegar dressing, use concentrated stock or
fruit or vegetable juice in place of some of
the oil.**

Spanish Beef Salad, Oriental Pork Salad,
Warm Minted Lamb Salad (pg 88)

CAESAR SALAD

Serves 4 as a light meal   **4g fat per serve**

80g reduced-fat and -salt ham
2 thick slices Italian (or rye) bread
1 cos lettuce, leaves separated
250g cherry tomatoes, halved
1 tablespoon thinly shaved fresh Parmesan
    cheese

CREAMY MUSTARD DRESSING
1 tablespoon low-fat mayonnaise
1/4 cup low-fat natural yoghurt
2 teaspoons wholegrain mustard
cracked black pepper to taste

Rinse ham under cold water to remove excess salt. Pat dry. Cut into thin strips. Heat a non-stick frying pan. Add ham. Cook for 5 minutes or until crisp. Drain and cool on kitchen paper.
Cut bread into cubes. Bake or grill until brown. Arrange lettuce leaves in a serving bowl. Top with tomatoes, bread, ham and Parmesan cheese. Drizzle over dressing.
Dressing: Place all ingredients in a bowl. Whisk to combine.

VEGETABLE RICE SALAD

Serves 8 as a side dish   **5g fat per serve**

4 cups cooked brown rice
2 Lebanese cucumbers, chopped
4 tomatoes, chopped
1/2 green capsicum, chopped
1/2 red capsicum, chopped
1 Spanish (red) onion, chopped
1/3 cup chopped fresh parsley
1/4 cup chopped fresh mint
2 tablespoons pine nuts (or slivered almonds)
juice of 2 limes (or lemons)
1 tablespoon olive oil
freshly ground black pepper to taste

Place all ingredients in a large bowl. Toss. Cover. Refrigerate for at least 1 hour before serving.

WARM MINTED LAMB SALAD

Serves 6 as a main meal   **6g fat per serve**

1/4 cup bottled mint jelly (or sauce)
1 tablespoon olive oil
1 clove garlic, crushed
2 tablespoons honey
1/2 teaspoon dried rosemary
700g lean lamb back straps (or leg steaks),
    trimmed of visible fat
4 cups (200g) mixed salad leaves
250g cherry tomatoes, halved
1 Lebanese cucumber, sliced

MINT CHUTNEY
3/4 cup low-salt chicken stock
1/4 cup apricot (or mango) chutney
2 tablespoons bottled mint jelly (or sauce)
1 tablespoon cider vinegar
2 tablespoons grated cucumber
1 tablespoon finely chopped Spanish (red) onion
2 teaspoons cornflour
1 tablespoon water

Combine mint jelly, oil, garlic, honey and rosemary in a bowl. Add lamb. Cover. Marinate in the refrigerator for at least 1 hour or overnight. Drain. Reserve marinade. Barbecue, grill or pan-fry lamb in a non-stick frying pan until brown on all sides and cooked as desired. Brush with reserved marinade during cooking. Cool slightly. Cut into thin slices. Arrange salad leaves, tomatoes and cucumber on a serving platter. Arrange lamb attractively over salad. Drizzle with a little mint chutney. Serve with remaining mint chutney and crusty bread.
Chutney: Combine stock, chutney, mint jelly, vinegar, cucumber and onion in a saucepan. Slowly bring to the boil. Combine cornflour and water with a little of the hot liquid. Gradually stir back into chutney. Reduce heat. Cook until slightly thickened.

Orange Coleslaw

Serves 4   **6g fat per serve**

2 large oranges, segmented, all white
    pith removed
2 cups shredded cabbage
1 cup chopped celery
1/2 red capsicum, thinly sliced
1/2 green capsicum, thinly sliced
2 tablespoons chopped walnuts
1/4 cup sultanas
1 large apple, grated
1 tablespoon lemon juice

ORANGE DRESSING
1/2 cup low-fat natural yoghurt
1 teaspoon grated orange rind
2 tablespoons orange juice
few drops Worcestershire sauce
1 tablespoon low-fat mayonnaise

Place all coleslaw ingredients in a bowl.
Toss. Add dressing. Toss again.
Dressing: Place all ingredients in a bowl.
Whisk to combine.

Cook's tip: For this slaw use all white, all
red or a combination of cabbages.

Salad Nicoise

Serves 6   **6g fat per serve**

200g green beans
1 butter (or mignonette) lettuce, leaves
    separated
1 radicchio lettuce, leaves separated
185g canned tuna slices in springwater, drained
125g cherry tomatoes, halved
8-10 black olives
2 hard-boiled eggs, roughly chopped (or
    quartered)

CREAMY DRESSING
1 clove garlic, crushed
freshly ground black pepper to taste
1/2 teaspoon Dijon mustard
1 tablespoon lemon juice
1 tablespoon olive oil
2 tablespoons buttermilk (or low-fat natural
    yoghurt)

Caesar Salad, Orange Coleslaw, Salad Nicoise, Waldorf
Grape Salad (pg 92)

Bring a saucepan of water to the boil. Add
beans. Cook for 2 minutes. Drain. Plunge
into cold water. Drain again.
Combine lettuce leaves in a serving bowl.
Arrange tuna, tomatoes, beans, olives and
eggs over lettuce. Drizzle with dressing.
Serve with Italian bread or baguettes.
Dressing: Place all ingredients in a jar.
Shake to combine.

Concentrate homemade stock by boiling down
to about one-sixth of its original volume.
Freeze in ice-cube trays for a handy flavour
boost in stir-fries, rice, dressings and sauces.
This concentrated stock is also useful to use
as a sauteeing baste or for brushing over
pastry. It can be rehydrated by adding boiling
water and then used as normal stock.

SPINACH AND MUSHROOM SALAD

Serves 2   **7.5g fat per serve**

2 cups baby spinach leaves
10 button mushrooms, sliced
10 cherry tomatoes, halved
1 tablespoon white wine (or balsamic) vinegar
2 teaspoons olive oil
2/3 cup (130g) low-fat cottage cheese
2 teaspoons pine nuts, toasted

Place spinach, mushrooms, tomatoes, vinegar and oil in a bowl. Toss. Arrange on a serving plate. Top with cottage cheese. Scatter with pine nuts. Serve with rye bread or crispbreads. *Recipe idea courtesy of Dairy Farmers*

MEDITERRANEAN PASTA SALAD

Serves 6   **10g fat per serve**

500g broccoli, chopped
250g elbow (or penne) pasta
2 teaspoons olive oil
250g button mushrooms, sliced
1 small onion, chopped
1 carrot, grated
250g cherry tomatoes, halved
1/2 red capsicum, sliced
freshly ground black pepper to taste

PESTO DRESSING

1 cup fresh basil leaves, finely chopped
1-2 cloves garlic, crushed
1 tablespoon grated Parmesan cheese
1/4 cup pine nuts
1 tablespoon olive oil
juice of 1 lemon

Boil or steam broccoli. Drain well.
Cook pasta in boiling water for 15-20 minutes or until tender. Drain. Rinse under cold water. Drain again.
Heat oil in a non-stick frying pan. Add mushrooms and onion. Cook until soft. Combine pasta, broccoli, mushroom mixture, carrot, tomatoes, capsicum and pepper in a bowl. Toss. Serve with dressing.
Dressing: Puree all ingredients in a blender.

SUMMER FISH SALAD

Serves 8 as a light meal   **7g fat per serve**

1/4 cup water
1/4 cup dry white wine
1 teaspoon dried oregano
500g salmon (gemfish, blue-eye cod, sea bream, leather-jacket, sea perch or ling) fillets, skin and bones removed, cut into bite-sized pieces
250g fresh scallops
1 cup seedless grapes
1 nectarine, cut into 8 wedges
3-4 cups (150-200g) mixed salad leaves

CREAMY ORANGE DRESSING

1/4 cup low-fat natural yoghurt
2 tablespoons orange juice
1 tablespoon chopped fresh chives
1 teaspoon chopped fresh dill
1 teaspoon chopped fresh ginger
freshly ground black pepper to taste

Combine water, wine and oregano in a saucepan. Bring to the boil. Reduce heat. Add fish. Simmer for 2-3 minutes or until almost cooked. Add scallops. Simmer for 1-2 minutes or until just cooked. Drain. Cool. Place salmon, scallops, grapes and nectarine in a bowl. Toss gently. To serve, arrange salad leaves on a serving platter. Top with salmon mixture. Spoon over dressing. Cover. Chill until ready to serve. Serve as a light meal with crusty bread or as an entree.
Dressing: Place all ingredients in a bowl. Whisk to combine.

Toasting nuts brings out their rich flavour. They are great for adding interest and flavour to rice and pasta dishes and salads. Remember nuts have a naturally high oil (poly- and monounsaturated) content, so don't go overboard with them.

Spinach and Mushroom Salad, Mediterranean Pasta Salad, Vegetable Rice Salad (pg 88)

Vegetable Couscous

Serves 8   **5g fat per serve**

1 tablespoon olive oil
$1/2$ onion, chopped
$1/2$ teaspoon cumin seeds
6 button mushrooms, sliced
1 carrot, finely chopped
1 zucchini, finely chopped
$1^1/4$ cups (250g) couscous
$1/2$ cup raisins (or currants)
2 cups boiling water (or stock)
2 tablespoons chopped fresh coriander
$1/3$ cup whole almonds, toasted

Heat half the oil in a heavy-based, high-sided, non-stick frying pan. Add onion and cumin seeds. Cook until soft. Add mushrooms, carrot and zucchini. Cook until tender. Stir in couscous and raisins. Pour over water. Cover pan with tight fitting lid. Stand for 10 minutes. Fluff up mixture with a fork. Stir in coriander and remaining oil. Serve sprinkled with almonds.

Waldorf Grape Salad

Serves 6   **8.5g fat per serve**

$1^1/2$ cups chopped celery
1 cup black grapes, halved
1 cup green grapes, halved
1 large red apple, chopped
$1/2$ cup walnuts
$1/3$ cup low-fat natural yoghurt
1 tablespoon lemon juice
1 tablespoon light sour cream (optional)

Place celery, grapes, apple and walnuts in a serving bowl. Toss. Place yoghurt, lemon juice and sour cream (if using) in a bowl. Whisk. Spoon dressing over salad. Toss.

Variation: For a more substantial salad add 2 cups chopped, cooked skinless chicken. For something a little different a pear can be used instead of the apple.
Nutrition note: When light sour cream is used the fat content of this recipe increases to 9.5g per serve.

Curried Kumara and Banana Salad

Serves 6   **3.5g fat per serve**

500g whole kumara (orange sweet potato), peeled
4 bananas, sliced
$1/4$ cup lemon (or lime) juice
2 spring onions, chopped
1 tablespoon canola oil
2 teaspoons mild curry powder
1 clove garlic, crushed
$1/2$ cup low-fat natural yoghurt
1 tablespoon chopped fresh parsley
1 tablespoon chopped fresh coriander

Boil or steam kumara. Cool. Cut into 2cm pieces. Combine bananas and lemon juice in a bowl. Add kumara and onions. Heat oil in a saucepan. Add curry powder and garlic. Cook until aromatic. Remove from heat. Combine curry mixture, yoghurt and half the parsley and coriander. Spoon over kumara mixture. Toss. Serve sprinkled with remaining parsley and coriander.

Glazed Carrots and Green Beans

Serves 4   **5.5g fat per serve**

4 baby carrots, cut into quarters
16 green beans
1 tablespoon honey
1 teaspoon wholegrain mustard
1 tablespoon low-salt chicken stock (or wine)
pinch ground ginger
freshly ground black pepper to taste
$1/4$ cup toasted slivered almonds

Boil or steam carrots and beans. Drain well. Return carrots and beans to pan. Combine honey, mustard, stock, ginger and pepper. Add to pan. Cook, stirring over low heat for 1-2 minutes or until vegetables are coated. Serve sprinkled with almonds.

Jellied Carrot And Pineapple Salad

Makes 8 slices   **4.5g fat per slice**

425g canned crushed pineapple in natural juice, drained, juice reserved
85g packet lemon jelly crystals (unsweetened if desired)
1 tablespoon cider vinegar
$^1/_2$ teaspoon ground ginger
1 cup grated carrot
$^1/_3$ cup chopped pecans (or walnuts)

Add enough water to the juice to make up to $1^1/_2$ cups. Place in a saucepan. Bring to the boil. Pour over the jelly crystals. Stir to dissolve. Stir in vinegar and ginger. Refrigerate until partially set. Fold in carrot, pineapple and nuts. Pour into a rinsed 4-cup (1 litre) capacity mould or individual moulds. Refrigerate until set. To serve, turn jelly onto a serving platter. Decorate with salad leaves, if desired.

Cook's tip: It is important that you do not use fresh pineapple for this recipe. Fresh pineapple contains enzymes which may prevent the jelly from setting.

Sweet And Sour Salad

Serves 6   **10g fat per serve**

2 tablespoons orange juice
1 tablespoon vinegar
1 tablespoon vegetable oil
freshly ground black pepper to taste
3 cups (150g) curly lettuce leaves
2 oranges, segmented
2 tomatoes, cut into wedges
2 fresh (or canned) peaches, sliced
2 carrots, cut into sticks
50g button mushrooms, sliced
$^1/_2$ cup whole almonds, toasted

Combine orange juice, vinegar, oil and pepper in a jar. Shake well. Tear lettuce leaves into pieces. Place in a bowl. Add oranges, tomatoes, peaches, carrots, mushrooms and almonds. Pour over dressing. Toss.

Sweet and Sour Salad, Fruity Rice Salad (pg 94),
Curried Kumara and Banana Salad,
Jellied Carrot and Pineapple Salad

Oven-roasted Tomatoes

neg fat

1kg Roma tomatoes, cut in half lengthways
2 tablespoons virgin olive oil
2 teaspoons chopped fresh basil
1 teaspoon chopped fresh oregano
$^1/_2$ teaspoon chopped fresh thyme
1 clove garlic, crushed
1 teaspoon ground pepper

Place tomatoes, skin-side down, on foil-lined baking trays. Combine remaining ingredients. Brush over tomatoes. Bake at 150°C for 2 hours or until roasted and slightly caramelised. Cook longer for drier tomatoes.

Cook's tip: Roma tomatoes are also known as egg, plum and Italian tomatoes.

Fruity Rice Salad

Serves 6   **3.5g fat per serve**

3 cups cooked brown rice
1 green apple, cored and chopped
425g canned peaches in natural juice, drained, juice reserved, chopped
1/2 cup diagonally sliced celery
1/2 cup chopped dried apricots
1/4 cup sultanas
2 green shallots, chopped
2 tablespoons pine nuts (or slivered almonds), toasted
1 tablespoon chopped fresh parsley
1 teaspoon grated orange rind

CREAMY MUSTARD DRESSING
2 tablespoons reserved peach juice
1 tablespoon white wine vinegar
2 tablespoons low-fat natural yoghurt
pinch mustard powder
freshly ground black pepper to taste

Place salad ingredients in a large bowl. Pour over dressing. Toss. Cover. Refrigerate until ready to serve.
Dressing: Place all ingredients in a bowl. Whisk to combine.

Stuffed Jacket Potatoes

Serves 4   **0.5g fat per serve**

4 large potatoes, scrubbed
filling of your choice (see Filling Ideas, following)

Pierce potatoes several times. Place on a baking tray. Bake at 180°C for 1 hour or until tender. Cut potatoes in half. Scoop out centre leaving a 1cm shell. Place flesh in a bowl. Mash. Add filling ingredients. Mix to combine. Spoon filling into potato shells. Bake at 180°C for 15 minutes or until browned.

Nutrition note: Fat content does include the filling.

Filling Ideas
• Cottage cheese, canned, no-added-salt salmon, drained and flaked and chopped spring onions.
• Chopped, cooked skinless chicken breast, sweet corn kernels, chopped red capsicum, curry paste and low-fat natural yoghurt.
• Cooked rice, grated pumpkin, grated zucchini, chopped fresh parsley and basil mashed with parsnip and ricotta cheese. Top potatoes with sesame and sunflower seeds.
• Lean cooked mince, chopped tomatoes, mushrooms and parsley. Top potatoes with grated reduced-fat mozzarella cheese.

Smoked Trout, Mango and Pasta Salad

Serves 4   **5g fat per serve**

1 cup penne pasta
1 small whole smoked trout, skin and bones removed, flesh flaked
1 large mango, sliced
2 tablespoons chopped fresh coriander
2 tablespoons chopped fresh parsley
juice of 1/2 lemon
2 green shallots, chopped
1 stick celery, chopped

YOGHURT MUSTARD DRESSING
1/4 cup low-fat natural yogurt
1 teaspoon mustard
juice of 1 lemon
1 tablespoon no-added-salt tomato sauce (or paste)
freshly ground black pepper to taste

Cook pasta in boiling water for 10 minutes or until tender. Drain well. Rinse under cold water. Drain again. Place pasta, trout, mango, coriander, parsley, lemon juice, shallots and celery in a large bowl. Toss. Drizzle with dressing. Toss.
Dressing: Place all ingredients in a bowl. Whisk to combine.

CARAMELISED WINTER VEGETABLES

Serves 6 as a side dish   **neg fat**

2 tablespoons sugar
2 fresh beetroot, peeled, chopped
1 Spanish (red) onion, chopped
1 turnip, chopped
1 carrot, chopped
1 parsnip, chopped
2 tablespoons water
$^1/_3$ cup pineapple (or apple) juice
2 tablespoons red wine (or cider) vinegar
freshly ground black pepper to taste
low-fat natural yoghurt

Sprinkle sugar over base of a large deep heavy-based frying pan. Cook over medium heat until sugar melts. Add beetroot, onion, turnip, carrot, parsnip, water, pineapple juice and vinegar. Cook over low heat for 15-20 minutes or until liquid evaporates. Season with pepper. Serve with yoghurt.

PUMPKIN AND CASHEW CURRY

Serves 4   **10g fat per serve**

2 teaspoons vegetable oil
1 onion, sliced
2 tablespoons chopped fresh coriander
1 teaspoon black (or yellow) mustard seeds
1 tablespoon mild curry powder
$^1/_2$ cup mango chutney
1 large tomato, chopped
4 zucchini, sliced
1 green capsicum, sliced
200g mushrooms, sliced
1 medium butternut pumpkin, peeled, chopped
50g raw cashews

Heat oil in a large saucepan. Add onion, coriander, mustard seeds and curry powder. Cook for 3-4 minutes. Stir in chutney, tomato, zucchini, capsicum, mushrooms and pumpkin. Cover. Cook over low heat for 30 minutes or until tender. Stir in cashews. Serve with brown rice and microwaved pappadams.

Cook's tip: Sauteeing spices before using will bring out extra flavour.

Summer Fish Salad (pg 90), Vegetable Couscous (pg 92), Smoked Trout, Mango and Pasta Salad

POTATO WEDGES

Serves 4 as a side dish   **5g fat per serve**

3 large pink-skinned potatoes, scrubbed
1 tablespoon vegetable (or olive) oil
seasoning of your choice such as dried
    rosemary leaves, sage, paprika or ground
    black pepper

Cut potatoes into wedges, French fries or chips. Place on sheets of kitchen paper. Blot to remove excess moisture. Place oil and seasoning in a bowl. Add potatoes. Toss to coat well. Place potatoes in a single layer on a greased baking tray. Bake at 220°C for 20 minutes. Loosen and turn wedges over. Bake for 10-15 minutes or until golden and crisp.

Cook's tip: For quicker cooking, boil or microwave potatoes until almost cooked. Pat dry. Proceed as directed in the recipe.

Vegetable au Gratin

Serves 6   **5.5g fat per serve**

4 leeks, trimmed, halved lengthways, cut into
    8cm pieces
8 baby carrots, peeled
8-12 fresh asparagus spears
2 tablespoons chopped walnuts
2 tablespoons reduced-fat mozzarella cheese

MUSTARD CHEESE SAUCE

1 tablespoon poly/monounsaturated margarine
1½ tablespoons plain flour
1¼ cups low-fat milk
3 teaspoons wholegrain mustard
⅓ cup grated reduced-fat mozzarella cheese

Boil or steam vegetables separately until just
cooked. Drain well. Arrange in an *au gratin*
dish. Pour over sauce. Sprinkle with walnuts
and cheese. Bake at 180°C for 5-10 minutes
or cook under a hot grill until golden. Serve
as a light meal with brown rice and grilled
tomatoes as an accompaniment.

Sauce: Melt margarine in a saucepan. Stir
in flour. Cook over a medium heat for 1 minute.
Remove from heat. Stir in milk. Cook,
stirring constantly, until sauce boils and
thickens. Stir in mustard and cheese. *Recipe
courtesy of Dairy Farmers, Farmers Best milk*

Orange Salad

Serves 6   **5g fat per serve**

3 oranges, segmented, reserve any juice
½ Spanish (red) onion, finely chopped
½ cucumber, finely chopped
¼ cup pecans
¼ cup black olives
¼ cup red wine (or balsamic) vinegar
1 teaspoon grated fresh ginger
1 bunch rocket
2 tablespoons chopped fresh mint

Combine oranges, onion, cucumber, pecans
and olives in a bowl. Place reserved orange
juice, vinegar and ginger in a small bowl.
Whisk to combine. Pour over salad. Toss.
Arrange rocket on a serving platter. Top with
salad. Sprinkle with mint.

Mushroom, Leek and Tomato Casserole

Serves 6   **6g fat per serve**

1 tablespoon olive oil
1 onion, chopped
1 clove garlic, crushed
125g button mushrooms, halved
3 leeks, sliced
2 tomatoes, peeled, chopped
freshly ground black pepper to taste
4 cups cooked brown rice
⅓ cup grated reduced-fat mozzarella (or low-
    fat tasty) cheese
⅓ cup fresh breadcrumbs (preferably made
    from 1-2 day old bread)
2 tablespoons chopped fresh parsley

Heat oil in a non-stick frying pan. Add onion
and garlic. Cook until soft. Add mushrooms,
leeks and tomatoes. Cook for 2-3 minutes.
Season with pepper. Spread rice over the
base of a greased high-sided casserole dish.
Top with mushroom mixture. Combine
cheese, breadcrumbs and parsley. Sprinkle
over mushroom mixture. Bake at 180°C for
5-10 minutes or until cheese melts and top is
lightly browned.

Hazelnut Rice Salad

Serves 4 as a side dish   **10g fat per serve**

1 cup wild rice blend
½ cup chopped fresh parsley
1 teaspoon grated lemon (or orange) rind
⅓ cup chopped roasted hazelnuts
½ cup chopped celery

HAZELNUT DRESSING

1 tablespoon hazelnut (or walnut, macadamia
    or extra virgin olive) oil
2 tablespoons raspberry (or red wine) vinegar
2 tablespoons orange juice
freshly ground black pepper to taste
½ teaspoon dried rosemary leaves

Boil or steam rice. Drain well. Place in a
bowl. Add remaining ingredients. Pour
dressing over warm rice mixture. Toss.
Cover. Refrigerate until well chilled.

Dressing: Combine all ingredients in a jar. Shake well.

Shopping tip: Wild rice blend is available from supermarkets. Hazelnut oil is available from delicatessens, health food stores and some supermarkets.

POTATO SALAD

Serves 6   **6g fat per serve**

6-8 (about 700 g) new (or pink-skinned) potatoes, unpeeled
$^1/_2$ cup chopped green shallots
2 tablespoons chopped fresh parsley
1 teaspoon chopped fresh mint (or $^1/_2$ teaspoon bottled mint sauce)
$^1/_2$ red capsicum, finely chopped
$^1/_3$ cup chopped walnuts

YOGHURT MUSTARD DRESSING

$^1/_3$ cup low-fat natural yoghurt
1 teaspoon dry (or Dijon) mustard
1 tablespoon lemon juice (or cider vinegar)
1 tablespoon evaporated skim (or low-fat) milk
1 teaspoon chopped fresh chives
1 tablespoon gherkin relish (optional)

Boil or steam potatoes until just cooked. Drain well. Cool. Chop. Place all ingredients, except nuts, in a bowl. Toss. Sprinkle with nuts.
Dressing: Place all ingredients in a small bowl and mix well.

TABBOULEH

Serves 6   **2g fat per serve**

1 cup burghul
$^1/_2$ cup finely chopped onion
1 cup chopped fresh parsley
$^1/_2$ cup chopped fresh mint
3 tomatoes, chopped

LEMON DRESSING

$^1/_3$ cup lemon juice
2 teaspoons olive oil
freshly ground black pepper to taste

Vegetable au Gratin, Pumpkin and Cashew Curry (pg 95), Mushroom, Leek and Tomato Casserole, Caramelised Winter Vegetables (pg 95)

Place burghul in a bowl. Cover with boiling water. Stand for 20 minutes or until burghul softens. Drain well. Press with the back of a spoon to remove excess moisture. Combine burghul, onion, parsley, mint and tomatoes in a bowl. Spoon over dressing. Toss.
Dressing: Place all ingredients in a jar. Shake well.

Cook's tip: Burghul is available from health food stores and most supermarkets.
Couscous Tabbouleh: Use couscous instead of burghul. Soak 1 cup couscous in 1 cup boiling water for 10-15 minutes. For a colour sensation, add $^1/_2$ cup grated carrot, 2 tablespoons currants and a few strips of finely sliced red capsicum.

97

DESSERTS

STICKY PEAR AND PARSNIP PUDDING WITH GINGER SYRUP

Makes 12 slices　　　　**9.5g fat per slice**

425g canned pears in natural juice, drained,
　　juice reserved
2 cups grated parsnip
$1/2$ cup ground almonds
$1^1/2$ cups self-raising flour
1 teaspoon bicarbonate of soda
$1/4$ cup firmly packed brown sugar
$1/4$ cup olive oil
$1/3$ cup buttermilk
2 eggs (or egg substitute)

GINGER SYRUP

$1/2$ cup reserved pear juice
2 tablespoons caster sugar
$1/2$ teaspoon ground ginger
1 tablespoon brandy (Cointreau or Grand
　　Marnier, optional)

Cut pears into thin slices. Combine pears, parsnip and almonds in a bowl. Sift flour and bicarbonate of soda into a bowl. Stir in pear mixture. Combine sugar, oil, buttermilk, eggs and 1 tablespoon reserved pear juice in a bowl. Beat until light and fluffy. Fold into flour mixture until just combined. Spoon mixture into a greased and lined 23cm round cake pan. Bake at 180°C for 50-55 minutes or until cooked when tested with a skewer. Stand in tin for 5 minutes. Turn onto a wire rack. Cool. Serve with Ginger Syrup and low-fat natural yoghurt or low-fat ice-cream.
Syrup: Place all ingredients in a saucepan. Cook, stirring, over low heat until sugar dissolves. Bring to the boil. Reduce heat. Simmer for 10 minutes or until slightly thickened.

CITRUS RICOTTA PUDDINGS WITH PEACH AND ORANGE SALSA

Serves 6　　　　**7.5g fat per serve**

$1^3/4$ cups (350g) ricotta cheese
1 cup low-fat natural yoghurt
1 egg
1 teaspoon grated lemon rind
1 teaspoon grated orange rind
2 teaspoons lemon juice
2 teaspoons orange juice
1 tablespoon sugar
1 teaspoon vanilla essence

PEACH AND ORANGE SALSA

2 large ripe peaches
1 orange
1 tablespoon marmalade
1 tablespoon rum (Cointreau or Grand Marnier)
2 tablespoons shredded fresh mint
1 tablespoon currants

Place ricotta cheese, yoghurt, egg, lemon and orange rind and juice, sugar and vanilla essence in a blender, food processor or electric mixer. Beat until smooth. Divide mixture between six $3/4$-cup (185mL) capacity ramekins. Place ramekins on a baking tray. Bake at 180°C for 25 minutes or until firm. Serve warm or cold with salsa.
Salsa: Finely chop peaches and orange. Place in a bowl. Add remaining ingredients. Toss. Serve at room temperature.

Citrus Ricotta Puddings with Peach and Orange Salsa,
Sticky Pear and Parsnip Pudding with Ginger Syrup

Rhubarb and Strawberry Crumble

Serves 8   **8g fat per serve**

1kg rhubarb, trimmed, cut into 3cm pieces
2 tablespoons sugar
2 tablespoons cornflour
1/3 cup water
500g strawberries, halved
1 teaspoon grated orange rind

CRUMBLE TOPPING

1/2 cup rolled oats
1/2 cup flaked almonds (or chopped walnuts)
2 tablespoons brown sugar
1 teaspoon ground cinnamon
1 tablespoon walnut (or sunflower) oil

Place rhubarb, sugar and cornflour in a greased 5-cup (1.25 litre) capacity ovenproof dish. Toss. Pour over water. Cover. Bake at 200°C for 20-30 minutes or until tender. Stir in strawberries and orange rind. Sprinkle with topping. Bake for 15-20 minutes or until topping is brown.
Topping: Combine oats, almonds, sugar and cinnamon in a bowl. Add oil. Mix well.

Fresh Apple Pudding

Serves 8   **15g fat per serve**

1 egg
1/4 cup sugar
1/3 cup vegetable oil
1 teaspoon vanilla essence
2 teaspoons grated orange rind
1/4 cup orange juice
3/4 cup self-raising flour
1/4 cup ground almonds
4 green apples, peeled, roughly chopped
2 teaspoons lemon juice
2 tablespoons brown sugar
1 teaspoon ground cinnamon
16 natural almonds

Place egg and sugar in a bowl. Beat until light and thick. Beat in oil, vanilla essence, orange rind and juice. Combine flour and ground almonds. Fold into egg mixture. Toss apples in lemon juice. Spread over base of a greased 20cm round or square ovenproof dish. Combine sugar and cinnamon. Sprinkle half over apples. Spread batter on top. Sprinkle with remaining sugar mixture. Press almonds into surface. Bake at 180°C for 35-40 minutes or until golden and pudding starts to come away from sides of dish. Serve warm with low-fat yoghurt or low-fat ice-cream.

F&P: Can be frozen for up to 2 months.

Apricot Mousse

Serves 6   **5g fat per serve**

1/3 cup chopped dried apricots
425g canned apricots in natural juice, drained, juice reserved
1/2 cup (100g) ricotta cheese
2 teaspoons gelatine
1/2 cup evaporated skim milk, well-chilled
2 tablespoons flaked almonds

Place dried apricots in a bowl. Cover with boiling water. Soak for 30 minutes or until soft. Drain.
Puree canned and soaked apricots and ricotta cheese in food processor. Transfer to a bowl. Place 1/4 cup reserved apricot juice in a bowl. Sprinkle over gelatine. Stand in hot water until gelatine dissolves. Stir into apricot mixture. Place milk in a bowl. Beat until thick and frothy. Fold into apricot mixture. Pour into 6 serving glasses or bowls. Refrigerate until set. To serve, decorate with almonds.

Cook and freeze fruit in season for adding to desserts, smoothies, salads and savoury dishes. Pureed cooked fruit adds flavour, sweetness and a moist texture to cakes and muffins. Try apples, pears, quinces, berries, peaches, plums and apricots.

Fresh Apple Pudding, Rhubarb and Strawberry Crumble

AMERICAN APPLE AND BLUEBERRY PIE

Makes 12 slices   **13g fat per slice**

4 green apples, peeled, chopped
2 tablespoons water
1 tablespoon lemon juice
1 teaspoon ground cinnamon
pinch ground cloves
1 quantity Sweet Almond Pastry (pg 138)
1 cup blueberries
2 tablespoons cornflour
low-fat milk for brushing

Combine apples, water, lemon juice, cinnamon and cloves in a saucepan. Cook over low heat until soft. Cool.
Roll out half the pastry to line a lightly greased 22cm pie dish. Gently ease into dish. Stir blueberries and cornflour into the apple mixture. Spoon into pastry case. Brush edges with milk. Roll out remaining pastry to cover pie. Gently place over pie. Trim edges. Press edges together by crimping with fingers. Lightly brush with milk. Bake at 180°C for 30 minutes or until golden.

CHOCOLATE CASSATA CREAM

Serves 8   **12g fat per serve**

1/2 cup raisins
1/4 cup dried apricots, chopped
1/3 cup rum
2 tablespoons cocoa
1 tablespoon icing sugar
1 tablespoon boiling water
2 1/2 cups (500g) ricotta cheese
1/3 cup evaporated skim milk
1/3 cup walnuts

BERRY SAUCE

300g fresh (or frozen, partially thawed)
    raspberries (or strawberries)
1 tablespoon Cointreau (or Grand Marnier,
    optional)
1 tablespoon icing sugar
1 tablespoon water

Combine raisins, apricots and rum in a bowl. Cover. Stand overnight. Combine cocoa, icing sugar and boiling water. Puree ricotta cheese, milk and cocoa mixture in a food processor. Add raisin mixture and walnuts. Pulse for 10 seconds or until just combined. Spoon mixture into 6 serving dishes. Cover. Refrigerate for least 6 hours or overnight. Serve with Berry Sauce and fresh fruit.
Sauce: Puree all ingredients in a food processor or blender.

FRESH FRUIT TARTLETS

Makes 24 tartlets   **7.5g fat per tartlet**

1 quantity Sweet Almond Pastry (pg 138)
3/4 cup (150g) ricotta cheese
2 tablespoons sugar
1 egg
1/4 cup evaporated skim milk
1/2 cup cooked white short-grain rice (or semolina)
fruit for decorating (e.g. blueberries,
    strawberries, peaches, mangoes, kiwi fruit)
1/4 cup apple and blackcurrant baby jelly,
    warmed

Roll out pastry to 3mm thick. Using a 7.5cm round fluted cutter, cut out 24 rounds. Gently ease pastry into greased muffin or patty pans. Prick all over with a fork. Line with foil or baking paper. Weigh down with uncooked rice. Bake at 190°C for 10 minutes. Remove rice and foil. Bake for 5-6 minutes or until golden. Cool.
Process ricotta cheese, sugar, egg and milk in food processor until light and smooth. Combine ricotta mixture and rice in a saucepan. Cook, stirring, over medium heat for 5-10 minutes or until mixture starts to thicken. Cool. Process in a food processor until smooth. Divide mixture between pastry cases. Top with fruit. Brush with warmed jelly. Chill until ready to serve.

Cook's tip: This recipe can also be made in a 23cm pie dish.

Date Tart (pg 104), American Apple and
Blueberry Pie, Chocolate Cassata Cream

DATE TART

Serves 8   **7.5g fat per serve**

8 sheets fillo pastry
2 tablespoons orange juice, approximately
1 teaspoon poly/monounsaturated margarine, melted
250g fresh (or packaged) dessert dates, pitted
2 egg yolks (or egg substitute)
2 tablespoons brown sugar
1 tablespoon cornflour
1¹/₂ cups low-fat milk
¹/₂ cup ground almonds
1 teaspoon vanilla essence
2 teaspoons grated orange rind

Brush pastry with orange juice. Layer into a 23cm pie dish. Trim leaving a 1.5cm edge. Brush edge with margarine. Arrange dates in pastry case. Combine egg yolks, sugar and cornflour in a bowl. Stir in milk, almonds, vanilla essence and orange rind. Pour over dates. Bake at 180°C for 30-40 minutes or until firm. Serve warm or cold with orange segments and low-fat ice-cream. *Recipe courtesy of Dairy Farmers, Farmers Best milk*

ITALIAN FRUIT TRIFLE

Serves 8   **6.5g fat per serve**

¹/₂ cup orange juice
2 tablespoons Cointreau (Grand Marnier or sweet sherry)
6-8 savoiardi sponge fingers biscuits
2 cups (400g) ricotta cheese
1 teaspoon vanilla essence
1 teaspoon grated orange rind
1 tablespoon orange juice, extra
2 teaspoons honey
pulp of 1 passionfruit
200g blueberries
2 oranges, segmented
125g strawberries, halved
2 fresh (or canned) peaches (or fruit of your choice), sliced
1 jar baby apple (or blackcurrant) jelly, warmed

Combine ¹/₂ cup orange juice and Cointreau in a bowl. Dip biscuits in mixture. Arrange in a serving dish.

Process ricotta cheese, vanilla essence, orange rind, extra orange juice and honey in a food processor until smooth. Fold in passionfruit pulp. Spoon over biscuits in bowl. Arrange fruit on top. Brush or spoon warm jelly over fruit.

Cook's tip: Savoiardi sponge fingers are Italian biscuits available from delicatessens and most supermarkets.

Author's note: This recipe was inspired by Belinda Jeffrey from *Better Homes and Gardens.*

CARAMEL ORANGES

Serves 8   **0.5g fat per serve**

6 large oranges
2 tablespoons sugar
1 tablespoon water

YOGHURT HONEY SAUCE

1 cup low-fat natural (or flavoured) yoghurt
1 cup (200g) low-fat cottage cheese
2 teaspoons grated orange rind
1 tablespoon Cointreau (Grand Marnier or orange juice)
1 tablespoon honey

Peel 1 orange. Cut rind into thin strips. Peel remaining oranges, removing all white pith. Cut oranges into 5mm thick slices. Arrange in a heatproof dish. Combine sugar, water and orange rind in a saucepan. Cook, stirring, over low heat until sugar dissolves. Bring to the boil. Boil until golden. Pour over oranges. Serve with sauce.

Sauce: Process all ingredients in a food processor until smooth. Alternatively, beat with an electric beater.

*Fresh Fruit Tartlets (pg 102),
Caramel Oranges, Apricot Mousse (pg 100)*

PINEAPPLE RICE PUDDING

Serves 8   **3g fat per serve**

1 cup (200g) ricotta cheese
200g low-fat natural yoghurt
1 teaspoon vanilla essence
2 cups drained, finely chopped, canned
    unsweetened pineapple
4 cups cooked white short-grain rice

Place ricotta cheese, yoghurt and vanilla essence in a bowl. Beat until creamy. Combine pineapple and rice. Fold into ricotta mixture. Spoon into a 6-cup (1.5 litre) capacity mould or individual moulds. Cover. Refrigerate for at least 4 hours. Just before serving, unmould. Serve with blueberries or strawberries, if desired.

RICH FRUIT DESSERT CAKE

Makes 12 slices   **5g fat per slice**

1 cup dried apricots, roughly chopped
1 cup pitted dates, roughly chopped
1 cup dried apples, roughly chopped
1 cup dessert figs, roughly chopped
1 tablespoon reduced-fat margarine
2 cups water
1 medium ripe banana, mashed
$1/2$ cup white self-raising flour
$1/2$ cup wholemeal self-raising flour
$1/2$ cup finely chopped walnuts
1 tablespoon finely grated orange rind

Combine apricots, dates, apples, figs, margarine and water in a saucepan. Bring to the boil. Reduce heat. Cover. Simmer for 5 minutes. Cool. Stir banana, flours, walnuts and orange rind into fruit mixture. Spoon mixture into a greased and lined 11 x 21cm loaf pan. Bake at 180°C for 40 minutes or cooked when tested with a skewer. Cool in pan. To serve, slice and accompany with low-fat yoghurt. *Recipe courtesy of Becel*

TROPICAL PAVLOVA

Serves 6   **1.5g fat per serve**

4 egg whites
pinch cream of tartar
$1/2$ cup sugar
1 teaspoon cornflour
$1/2$ teaspoon white vinegar
$1/2$ teaspoon vanilla essence
1 tablespoon cold water
150g low-fat fruche (or fromage frais – not
    pineapple)
$1/3$ cup (65g) ricotta cheese
1 mango, sliced
2 kiwi fruit, sliced
125g strawberries, sliced
1 banana, sliced
pulp of 2 passionfruit

Cover a baking tray with baking paper. Mark a 20cm circle.
Beat egg whites and cream of tartar in a bowl until soft peaks form. Gradually beat in half the sugar. Combine cornflour and remaining sugar. Gradually beat into egg whites. Beat until thick and glossy. Fold in vinegar, vanilla essence and water. Spoon onto prepared tray. Make a slight hollow in the centre. Bake at 150°C on lowest shelf of oven for $1^1/2$ hours or until crisp and dry to touch. Cool in oven with door ajar.
Beat together fruche and ricotta cheese. Just before serving, top pavlova with fruche mixture. Decorate with fruit. Drizzle with passionfruit.

Cook's tip: Any fresh or canned unsweetened fruit of your choice can be used to decorate the pavlova.

When cooking rice, cook more than you need and freeze or use next day for salads, stuffings, soups and casseroles or pureed in desserts for sweetening and thickening. Great also as a quick accompaniment to stir-fries.

COFFEE HAZELNUT TERRINE

Serves 8   **5g fat per serve**

1 tablespoon gelatine
2 tablespoons water
1 cup boiling strong coffee (use decaffeinated if
    you prefer)
$^1/_4$ cup sugar

HAZELNUT LAYER

1 tablespoon gelatine
$^1/_4$ cup water
$^1/_2$ cup evaporated skim milk, well-chilled
$^3/_4$ cup (150g) ricotta cheese
2 tablespoons coffee creme liqueur
1 teaspoon vanilla essence
1 teaspoon honey
2 tablespoons evaporated skim milk, extra
$^1/_4$ cup ground hazelnuts

Sprinkle gelatine over water. Stand in hot water until gelatine dissolves. Add coffee and sugar. Stir until sugar dissolves. Cool. Pour into rinsed 4-cup (1 litre) capacity rectangular dish or mould. Refrigerate until set.
Gently pour hazelnut layer over coffee layer. Refrigerate until set. Just before serving unmould terrine. Slice.
Hazelnut Layer: Sprinkle gelatine over water. Stand in hot water until gelatine dissolves. Gradually stir in $^1/_2$ cup milk. Beat ricotta in a separate bowl until light and fluffy. Beat in coffee liqueur, vanilla essence, honey and extra milk. Fold in gelatine mixture and hazelnuts.

Desserts do not have to be sweetened with sugar. Try pureed or mashed ripe fruit, fruit juice concentrate, rehydrated dried fruit (with liquid). Nuts, rice and wholegrains also add natural sweetness, flavour and texture.

Top: Italian Fruit Trifle (pg 104), Coffee Hazelnut Terrine, Tropical Pavlova
Bottom: Rich Fruit Dessert Cake, Pineapple Rice Pudding

Summer Berry Pudding

Serves 6 **1.5g fat per serve**

3 cups fresh (or frozen) mixed berries (e.g. blueberries, strawberries and raspberries)
1/4 cup water
1/2 loaf (10-12 slices) white (or wholemeal) sliced bread, crusts trimmed
85g packet port wine (or raspberry) jelly crystals (diabetic if preferred)

Combine 1 cup of berries and water in a saucepan. Cook for 2-3 minutes or until heated. Mash roughly. Line a 4-cup (1 litre) capacity bowl or mould with about three-quarters of the bread. Overlap slices so there are no gaps. Pour berry mixture over bread, pressing down lightly. Fill with remaining berries.
Make up jelly according to packet directions, using only one-half the recommended water. Pour three-quarters of the jelly over berries. Top with remaining bread. Pour over remaining jelly. Cover with plastic wrap. Place a plate on top with a heavy weight on it. Refrigerate overnight. To serve, unmould pudding onto a serving platter and accompany with low-fat ice-cream or low-fat natural yoghurt.

Passionfruit Frozen Yoghurt

Serves 4-6 **nil fat**

1 teaspoon gelatine
2 tablespoons water
200g low-fat flavoured yoghurt (e.g. mango, peach or apricot)
1 egg white
pulp of 2 passionfruit

Sprinkle gelatine over water. Stand in hot water until gelatine dissovles. Combine yoghurt and gelatine. Stir to combine. Pour into a shallow freezerproof dish. Freeze until firm. Transfer to a bowl. Beat until doubled in volume. Beat egg white until stiff peaks form. Fold into yoghurt mixture with passionfruit. Refreeze. Remove from freezer 5 minutes before serving. Serve with fresh fruit and mint, if desired.

To make low-fat yoghurt thick and creamy, place in a sieve lined with muslin and leave in the refrigerator overnight to drain. This is great to use in desserts or for replacing sour cream on baked potatoes, in dressings, dips and sauces.

Summer Berry Pudding, Passionfruit Frozen Yoghurt

CREPES

Makes 8-10 crepes **2g fat per crepe**

1 cup plain flour
1 whole egg (or 2 egg whites)
1¼ cups low-fat milk
½ teaspoon vanilla essence (optional)
vegetable oil spray (or vegetable oil)

Process flour in a food processor for 10 seconds. Combine, egg, milk and vanilla essence (if using). With motor running pour into flour. Process until smooth. Stand for 15-20 minutes. Heat a non-stick frying pan. Lightly spray with oil. Pour 2-3 tablespoons of batter in pan. Cook until lightly browned on the base. Turn crepe. Cook until brown on second side. Repeat with remaining batter.

Nutrition note: Fat content is for unfilled crepes.

French Lemon Crepes: Place grated rind and juice of 2 lemons, 2 tablespoons marmalade and ³/4 cup water in a saucepan. Heat. Blend 1 tablespoon cornflour with ¹/4 cup water and a little of the hot liquid from pan. Stir into pan. Cook, stirring, until sauce boils and thickens. Fill crepes with vanilla fromage frais or fruche. Top with sauce.

Tangy Apple and Cinnamon: Add 1 teaspoon grated orange rind to crepe batter. Place 2 large grated green apples, ¹/2 cup fresh orange juice and 2 tablespoons sultanas in a saucepan. Heat for 2-3 minutes or until mixture is hot. Blend 1 teaspoon cornflour with 1 tablespoon water. Stir into apple mixture. Cook, stirring, until mixture boils and thickens. Fill crepes with mixture. Sprinkle with ground cinnamon. Serve with low-fat yoghurt or ricotta cheese, if desired.

Tropical Crepes: Combine 1 cup low-fat cottage cheese, ¹/4 cup crushed unsweetened pineapple and 1 tablespoon chopped fresh mint in a bowl. Place a spoonful of mixture on each crepe. Top with sliced peaches. Sprinkle with a few chopped macadamia nuts and a little ground nutmeg. Roll crepes to enclose filling. Drizzle with passionfruit pulp.

Brandied Prune and Ricotta: Combine 1 cup sliced, pitted brandied prunes and 2 tablespoons water in a saucepan. Heat for 5 minutes. Cool slightly. Combine 1 cup ricotta cheese and undrained prunes in a bowl. Fill crepes with mixture. Sprinkle with toasted flaked almonds.

Strawberry Ricotta: Fill crepes with Strawberry Ricotta Cream (pg 122).

Maple Banana and Walnut: Slice 3 bananas, diagonally. Place in a bowl. Add 2 teaspoons lemon juice. Toss. Heat ¹/3 cup maple syrup in a saucepan. Stir in ¹/4 cup roughly chopped walnuts and the bananas. Cook over low heat until bananas are heated. For Jamaican bananas use 2 tablespoons rum and 2 tablespoons brown sugar instead of the maple syrup.

Be creative and experiment with your own ideas – use fruit, yoghurt, ricotta or cottage cheese or simply layer with a sprinkle of lemon juice and a drizzle of honey.

Clockwise from top: Strawberry Ricotta Crepes, Maple Banana and Walnut Crepes, Tangy Apple and Cinnamon Crepes

BAKING

Orange Semolina Cake

Makes 25 diamonds   **5.5g fat per diamond**

1 cup low-fat natural yoghurt
1/2 teaspoon baking powder
1/3 cup extra virgin olive oil
1 tablespoon honey
1 cup semolina
1/2 cup ground almonds
1/4 cup sugar
1/4 cup currants
1 teaspoon grated orange rind
1/4 cup pine nuts
2 tablespoon apricot jam (or marmalade)
1/4 cup orange blossom water

Combine yoghurt and baking powder in a bowl. Stand for 15 minutes. Add oil and honey. Combine next 5 ingredients. Stir into yoghurt mixture. Spread evenly into a greased and lined 20cm square cake pan. Sprinkle with pine nuts. Mark into 3-4cm diamond shapes. Bake at 180°C for 40 minutes or until golden. Combine jam and orange water. Remove cake from oven. Immediately run a knife along marked lines. Pour jam mixture over hot cake. Bake for 5 minutes. Cool in pan.

F&P: Can be frozen for up to 3 months.
Variation: For a lemon flavoured cake, use 2 tablespoons lemon juice and 1 tablespoon brown sugar in place of the jam and orange blossom water.

Almond Biscotti

Makes 30 slices   **2.5g fat per slice**

1 2/3 cups plain flour
1/2 teaspoon baking powder
2 large eggs
1/2 cup caster sugar
1 teaspoon vanilla essence
1 teaspoon grated orange rind
3/4 cup blanched almonds, lightly toasted
egg white

Sift together flour and baking powder into a

bowl. In a separate bowl, beat eggs, sugar, vanilla essence and orange rind until thick and creamy. Fold egg mixture and almonds into flour mixture. Knead on a floured surface to a firm dough. Divide dough in half. Shape each piece into a log about 5cm wide and 3cm thick. Place on a greased and floured baking tray. Brush with egg white. Bake at 180°C for 30 minutes or until firm. Cool for 10 minutes. Cut each log diagonally into 1cm thick slices. Place on baking trays. Bake at 160°C for 20-30 minutes or until dry and crisp. Cool on wire racks. Store in an airtight container.

Variation: Hazelnuts, pistachios, dried and glace fruit can be used instead of almonds.

Cinnamon Nut Cigars

Makes 36 cigars   **2.5g fat per cigar**

1/4 cup walnuts, roughly chopped
1 tablespoon brown sugar
2 teaspoons ground cinnamon
6 sheets fillo pastry
2 tablespoons light olive (or canola) oil
     for brushing
1/4 cup pine nuts
egg white

Combine walnuts, sugar and cinnamon in a bowl. Layer 2 sheets of pastry with short side facing you. Lightly brush lower half of pastry with oil. Sprinkle with one-third of the nut mixture. Fold pastry in half. Lightly brush with oil. Sprinkle with one-third of the pine nuts. Cut into three strips lengthways, then cut each strip in half. Roll up. Place seam side down on a greased baking tray. Lightly brush with egg white. Repeat with remaining pastry, nut mixture and pine nuts. Bake at 180°C for 10-12 minutes or until golden. Cool on a wire rack.

Orange Semolina Cake, Hazelnut Macaroons (pg 116),
Cinnamon Nut Cigars, Almond Biscotti

GRAN'S FESTIVE CAKE

Makes 20 slices   **6g fat per slice**

1/2 cup red glace cherries, halved
1/2 cup chopped glace pineapple
1 cup chopped mixed peel
1/4 cup glace ginger
3/4 cup chopped pecans (or walnuts)
1/2 cup self-raising flour
1/2 cup plain flour
2 tablespoons poly/monounsaturated
    margarine, softened
1/3 cup sugar
2 eggs
1/4 cup unsweetened pineapple juice
1 tablespoon rum (optional)
apricot jam, warmed and sieved (optional)
halved pecans (or walnuts, optional)

Combine first 5 ingredients. Sift together flours. Add 2 tablespoons flour to fruit mixture. Toss. Beat margarine, sugar and eggs until light and creamy. Fold in remaining flour mixture, alternately, with pineapple juice. Fold in fruit mixture. Spoon mixture into a greased and lined 10 x 20cm loaf pan. Bake at 160°C for 1¼ hours or until cooked when tested with a skewer. Sprinkle with rum (if using), brush with jam and decorate with pecans (if using).

F&P: Can be frozen for up to 12 months.
Author's note: This recipe from my late grandmother is an old favourite which I have adapted. It is a great cake to serve at Christmas, for special occasions or just as a morning tea treat.

MARZIPAN

Makes 20 slices   **4g fat per slice**

1 cup ground almonds
1/3 cup pure icing sugar
1/4 cup caster sugar
3 teaspoons egg white (about half 1 egg white)
1/4 teaspoon almond essence (or 1/2 teaspoon
    amaretto liqueur)
few drops orange blossom water (or pure
    vanilla essence)

Sift almonds and sugars into a bowl. Add egg

white, almond essence and orange water. Mix to make a smooth stiff paste. Wrap in plastic wrap. Chill until required. This recipe makes a 4 x 10cm log. Roll out or cut and use as desired.

Cook's tip: When rolling out marzipan, dust the surface with a little pure icing sugar or ground almonds to prevent it from sticking. Dust with icing sugar before chilling.

MARZIPAN TRIANGLES

Makes 42 triangles   **7g fat per triangle**

1 cup rolled oats
1/2 cup caster sugar
1 cup self-raising flour, sifted
3/4 cup ground almonds
1 tablespoon golden syrup
1/2 cup canola oil
1 egg
1/4 teaspoon almond essence
1/2 quantity marzipan (this page)
1/3 cup chopped almonds for decoration

Combine oats, sugar, flour and ground almonds in a bowl. Combine golden syrup, oil, egg and almond essence. Stir into oats mixture. Spread half the mixture evenly over base of a greased and lined 20 x 30cm lamington pan. Roll out marzipan to cover. Place over oats mixture. Top with remaining oats mixture. Sprinkle with chopped almonds. Press into mixture. Bake at 180°C for 30 minutes or until golden. Stand for 10 minutes. Cut into triangles.

Do not be misled by claims on labels such as 'reduced' and 'light'. They do not necessarily mean that the food is low in fat. Read nutrition panels and compare brands to find the one lowest in fat – or look for the Heart Foundation's Tick of Approval.

Irish Barmbrack (pg 122), Coffee Delights (pg 116), Marzipan, Marzipan Triangles, Gran's Festive Cake

Peanut Butter and Honey Cookies

Makes 30 cookies   **4.5g fat per cookie**

³/4 cup crunchy, no-added-salt peanut butter
²/3 cup honey
1 egg, lightly beaten
1 cup plain flour, sifted
¹/2 cup rolled oats
¹/3 cup sultanas

Place peanut butter and honey in a saucepan. Cook, stirring, over low heat until soft and combined. Cool slightly. Stir in egg. Fold in remaining ingredients. Shape teaspoons of mixture into balls. Place on paper-lined baking trays. Press lightly with a fork. Bake at 160°C for 12 minutes or until golden. Cool on wire racks.

F&P: Can be frozen for up to 3 months.

Apricot Wheat Germ Loaf

Makes 16 slices   **4.5g fat per slice**

2 cups wheat germ
2 cups low-fat milk
²/3 cup chopped dried apricots
³/4 cup lightly packed brown sugar
2 tablespoons honey
2 cups wholemeal self-raising flour, sifted
¹/2 cup chopped walnuts

Place wheat germ in a bowl. Pour over milk. Stir in remaining ingredients. Spoon into a greased and lined 10 x 20cm loaf pan. Bake at 180°C for 55-60 minutes or until cooked when tested with a skewer. Stand for 5 minutes. Turn onto a wire rack. Cool.

F&P: Can be frozen for up to 3 months.

Coffee Delights

Makes 20 pieces   **nil fat**

1 tablespoon gelatine
2 tablespoons water
1 cup boiling strong coffee
2 tablespoons sugar

Sprinkle gelatine over water. Stand in hot water until gelatine dissolves. Stir in coffee and sugar. Stir until dissolved. Cool. Pour into a rinsed 20cm square cake pan. Refrigerate until set. Cut into fingers or squares.

Hazelnut Macaroons

Makes 20   **5.5g fat per macaroon**

2 egg whites
¹/2 cup icing sugar, sifted
1 cup ground hazelnuts
1 teaspoon finely grated orange rind
¹/4 cup flaked almonds

Beat egg whites until soft peaks form. Combine remaining ingredients. Fold into egg whites. Place spoonfuls of mixture on paper-lined baking trays. Bake at 200°C for 10-12 minutes or until golden. Cool on wire racks.

Ginger Biscuits

Makes 28 biscuits   **1.5g fat per biscuit**

2 tablespoons poly/monounsaturated margarine
2 tablespoons sugar
1 egg
¹/2 cup wholemeal plain flour, sfited
¹/2 cup white plain flour, sifted
1 teaspoon ground ginger
1 tablespoon glace ginger
¹/2 teaspoon ground nutmeg
¹/4 teaspoon ground cloves
1 tablespoon molasses (or golden syrup),
    warmed

Beat margarine and sugar in a bowl until light and fluffy. Beat in egg. Stir in remaining ingredients. Cover. Refrigerate for 1 hour. Roll teaspoons of mixture into balls. Place on lightly greased baking trays. Flatten slightly with a fork. Bake at 160°C for 10-12 minutes or until golden.

F&P: Can be frozen baked or the unbaked dough can be formed into a log and frozen.

Ginger Biscuits, Peanut Butter and
Honey Cookies, Apricot Wheat Germ Loaf

Glazed Banana and Mango Cake

Makes 12 slices   **6g fat per slice**

425g canned sliced mango in natural juice, drained, juice reserved
1 1/2 cups white self-raising flour
1/2 cup wholemeal self-raising flour
1 teaspoon bicarbonate of soda
1 teaspoon mixed spice
1/4 cup brown sugar
60g poly/monounsaturated margarine
1 egg
1/2 cup buttermilk
3 ripe bananas, mashed
1 teaspoon vanilla essence
2 tablespoons flaked almonds

MANGO GLAZE
2/3 cup icing sugar
1 tablespoon low-fat natural yoghurt
1/2 teaspoon grated lemon rind
1/2 teaspoon lemon juice
30g reserved mango flesh

Slice mangoes thickly. Reserve 30g mango flesh for glaze.
Sift flours, bicarbonate of soda and mixed spice into a bowl. In a separate bowl, beat sugar and margarine until light and creamy. Gradually beat in egg and buttermilk. Add bananas, vanilla essence and 1 tablespoon reserved mango juice. Beat until just combined. Fold in flour mixture, take care not over mix. Spread one-third of the batter over base of a greased and floured 20cm round cake pan. Top with half the mangoes, leaving a 1-2cm border. Spread with another one-third of the batter. Cover with remaining mangoes. Spread with remaining batter. Sprinkle with almonds. Bake at 180°C for 50-60 minutes or until cooked when tested with a skewer. Stand for 10 minutes. Turn onto a wire rack to cool. Brush with mango glaze.
Glaze: Puree all ingredients in a food processor. Push through a seive.

F&P: Can be frozen for up to 3 months.

Carrot and Walnut Cake

Makes 18 slices   **9g fat per slice**

1 3/4 cups white self-raising flour
2/3 cup wholemeal self-raising flour
1/2 teaspoon bicarbonate of soda
2 teaspoons mixed spice
1/2 teaspoon ground nutmeg
1/2 cup sultanas
1/2 cup chopped walnuts
1/2 cup brown sugar
1/4 cup light olive (or canola) oil
2 eggs
2/3 cup buttermilk
2 teaspoons vanilla essence
1 1/2 cups grated carrot
225g canned crushed pineapple in natural juice, undrained
double quantity Lemon Yoghurt Icing (page 138)
1/3 cup chopped walnuts, extra

Sift together flours, bicarbonate of soda, mixed spice and nutmeg into a bowl. Add sultanas and walnuts. In a separate bowl, beat sugar and oil until light and fluffy. Beat in eggs, one at a time. Stir in buttermilk and vanilla essence. Fold in flour mixture, carrot and pineapple. Pour mixture into greased and lined 28cm round cake pan. Bake at 180°C for 20-25 minutes or until cooked when tested with a skewer. Stand for 5 minutes. Turn onto a wire rack to cool. Spread cold cake with Lemon Yoghurt Icing (pg 138). Sprinkle with extra walnuts.

F&P: Can be frozen without icing for up to 3 months.

Light olive oil does not mean that the oil is light in fat, it refers to the flavour of the oil. All olive and other oils are close to 100% fat as are butter and margarine, but their composition, flavour and uses differ.

Tangy Fruit Loaf

Makes 16 slices   **8g fat per slice**

1/4 cup canola (or vegetable) oil
1/2 cup brown sugar
1 egg
3 bananas, sliced
1/2 cup pitted dates
1/4 cup lemon juice
1 1/2 cups wholemeal plain flour, sifted
1/2 cup wheat germ
1/2 teaspoon baking powder
1/2 teaspoon bicarbonate of soda
1/2 cup chopped pecans

Beat oil and sugar until thick and foamy. Beat in egg. Stir in bananas, dates and lemon juice. Combine flour, wheat germ, baking powder, bicarbonate of soda and pecans. Fold into banana mixture. Spoon mixture into a greased and lined 8 x 20cm loaf pan. Bake at 160°C for 50-60 minutes or until cooked when tested with a skewer. Stand for 5 minutes. Turn onto a wire rack. Cool.

F&P: Can be frozen for up to 3 months.
Variations: Use any of the following in place of the banana, dates and lemon juice: 1 cup stewed apple, 1 cup sultanas, 1 teaspoon ground cinnamon; 1 cup dried apricots soaked in water overnight and 1/4 cup liquid; 3/4 cup low-fat natural yoghurt, 1 teaspoon ground cinnamon, grated lemon rind; 3/4 cup unsweetened orange juice, 2 tablespoons grated orange rind.

Walnut Chocolate Slice

Makes 25 pieces   **2g fat per piece**

4 egg whites
1/4 cup sugar
1/2 cup canned unsweetened pie apple
1/2 cup low-fat milk
1 1/2 teaspoons vanilla essence
1 cup plain flour
1/4 cup brown sugar
1/3 cup cocoa powder
2 teaspoons baking powder
1/2 teaspoon bicarbonate of soda
1/3 cup chopped walnuts (or pecans)

Beat egg whites until soft peaks form. Gradually beat in sugar. Beat until sugar dissolves. Fold in apple, milk and vanilla essence. Sift together flour, brown sugar, cocoa, baking powder and bicarbonate of soda into a large bowl. Make a well in the centre. Fold in egg whites until just combined. Spoon into a greased and lined 23cm square slab pan. Sprinkle with walnuts. Bake at 190°C for 20-25 minutes or until cooked when tested with a skewer. Cool in pan. Cut into 4-5cm squares. Serve with fresh berries or Strawberry Ricotta Cream (pg 122), if desired.

F&P: Can be frozen for up to 3 months.

Fruit Ring

Makes 12 slices   **4g fat per slice**

1 cup white self-raising flour
1 cup wholemeal self-raising flour
1 teaspoon baking powder
1 tablespoon brown sugar
2 tablespoons olive (or vegetable) oil
1 cup buttermilk
1 tablespoon low-fat milk
1/2 teaspoon mixed spice
1 teaspoon sugar

SPICY SULTANA FILLING
1/2 cup sultanas
1 teaspoon grated lemon rind
1/4 cup currants
1 teaspoon ground cinnamon
2 tablespoons brown sugar

Sift dry ingredients into a bowl. Make a well in the centre. Combine oil and buttermilk. Pour into well. Mix to a soft dough. Roll out dough to make a 15 x 35cm rectangle. Spread with filling leaving a 2.5cm border. Roll up lengthways. Shape into a ring. Place on a lightly greased baking tray. Make 2.5cm deep cuts in dough at 2.5cm intervals. Brush with milk. Sprinkle with mixed spice and sugar. Bake at 180°C for 35 minutes or until golden.
Filling: Combine all ingredients in a bowl.

F&P: Can be frozen for up to 3 months.

Clockwise from top: Tangy Fruit Loaf, Walnut Chocolate Slice, Ricotta and Ginger Roll (pg 122)

Irish Barmbrack

Makes 40 slices   **1.5g fat per slice**

1$^1/_2$ cups cold black tea
1$^1/_4$ cups sultanas
1 cup currants
$^3/_4$ cup mixed peel, finely chopped
$^1/_2$ cup brown sugar
1 egg, lightly beaten
2 cups self-raising flour, sifted
$^1/_2$ cup walnuts (almonds or brazil nuts)

Combine tea, sultanas, currants, mixed peel and sugar in a bowl. Cover. Stand overnight. Stir in egg. Mix in flour and walnuts. Spoon into a greased and lined 13 x 21cm loaf pan. Bake at 160°C for 1-1$^1/_4$ hours or until cooked when tested with a skewer. Stand for 5 minutes. Turn onto a wire rack to cool.

F&P: Can be frozen for up to 3 months.

Ricotta and Ginger Roll

Makes 10 slices   **4.5g fat per slice**

4 eggs (or egg substitute)
$^1/_2$ cup caster sugar
$^1/_2$ cup plain flour, sifted
1 teaspoon ground cinnamon
1 teaspoon ground nutmeg
1 teaspoon ground allspice
4 egg whites
1 tablespoon golden syrup

RICOTTA AND GINGER FILLING

2$^1/_4$ cups (250g) ricotta cheese
40g glace ginger, chopped
$^1/_4$ cup glace cherries, chopped

Beat eggs and sugar until pale and thick. Fold in flour and spices. Beat egg whites in a separate bowl until soft peaks form. Gradually beat in golden syrup. Continue beating until stiff peaks form. Fold into flour mixture. Spoon mixture into a greased and lined 26 x 32cm Swiss roll pan. Bake at 180°C for 15 minutes or until cake springs back when gently pressed with fingertips. Immediately turn onto a sheet of baking paper sprinkled with caster sugar. Roll up.

Stand until cold. Unroll cake. Remove paper. Spread with filling. Firmly reroll. Serve with crystallised ginger, if desired.
Filling: Beat ricotta cheese until smooth and creamy. Stir in ginger and cherries.

Light Devonshire Tea

Makes 10 scones   **4g fat per scone**

2 cups self-raising flour, sifted
1 tablespoon poly/monounsaturated (or canola) margarine
1 cup low-fat milk (or buttermilk)
1 tablespoon strawberry (or raspberry) jam

STRAWBERRY RICOTTA CREAM

125g strawberries
$^3/_4$ cup (150g) ricotta cheese

Place flour into a bowl. Rub in margarine until mixture resembles fine breadcrumbs. Make a well in the centre. Pour in milk, keeping a little for glazing. Mix quickly with a knife to make a soft dough. Knead dough, quickly, on a lightly floured surface until smooth. Press or roll to 2cm thick. Cut out rounds, using a 6cm cutter. Place on a greased baking tray. Brush lightly with milk. Bake at 210-220°C for 8-10 minutes or until golden. Serve with jam and strawberry cream.
Strawberry cream: Puree strawberries in a food processor. Add ricotta cheese and process to combine.

F&P: Scones can be frozen for up to 3 months.
Cook's tip: For low-fat scones, cakes and biscuits which are extra light and fluffy use buttermilk rather than milk. This works especially well when using wholemeal flour.

From top: Fruit Ring (pg 120), Light Devonshire Tea, Tea Wedges with Orange Ricotta Cream (pg 124)

The Keane gang!

14 May 2010

Tea Wedges with Orange Ricotta Cream

Makes 10 wedges   **6.5g fat per wedge**

1$^3/_4$ cups self-raising flour, sifted
2 tablespoon sugar
1 teaspoon ground cinnamon
40g poly/monounsaturated margarine, melted
1 teaspoon grated orange rind
$^1/_2$ cup buttermilk
1 egg
$^1/_2$ teaspoon vanilla essence
$^1/_3$ cup sultanas

ORANGE RICOTTA CREAM

1 cup (200g) ricotta cheese
1 teaspoon grated orange rind
$^1/_4$ teaspoon vanilla essence
1 tablespoon icing sugar
1 tablespoon orange juice

Combine flour, sugar and cinnamon in a bowl. Make a well in the centre. Combine remaining ingredients. Pour into well. Mix to make a soft dough. Lightly knead dough until smooth. Pat out to make a 20cm circle. Cut into 10 wedges. Place on a lightly greased baking tray. Bake at 190°C for 15-20 minutes or until golden. Serve with Orange Ricotta Cream.
Ricotta Cream: Place all ingredients in a bowl. Beat.

F&P: Wedges can be frozen for up to 3 months.

For a low-fat alternative to cream on any occasion, whip ricotta with any fruit or rehydrated dried fruit and flavour with a few drops of vanilla essence or liqueur.

Mixed Seed Bread

Makes 20 slices   **3.5g fat per slice**

$^1/_3$ cup linseed
$^1/_3$ cup burghul
$^2/_3$ cup boiling water
1 tablespoon (2 sachets) dried yeast
1 tablespoon sugar
2 cups warm water
$^1/_4$ cup sunflower seeds
$^1/_4$ cup sesame seeds
2 cup wholemeal plain flour
1$^1/_2$ cups white plain flour
extra sesame (or poppy) seeds

Combine linseed, burghul and boiling water in a bowl. Soak for 20 minutes. Drain off unabsorbed water. Dissolve yeast and sugar in $^1/_2$ cup of warm water. Stand in a warm place for 10 minutes or until frothy.
Combine remaining dry ingredients, except the extra seeds, in a bowl. Stir in yeast mixture. Mix in remaining warm water to make a soft dough. Knead on a lightly floured surface for 5-7 minutes or until smooth. Add more flour if necessary. Place in a lightly oiled bowl. Turn to coat with oil. Cover. Stand in a warm place for about 1 hour or until doubled in size. Punch down. Knead for 2 minutes. Shape into a loaf. Place in a lightly greased 13 x 21cm loaf pan. Sprinkle with extra sesame seeds. Dust with flour. Bake at 190-200°C for 40 minutes or until bread sounds hollow when tapped.

F&P: Can be frozen for up to 2 months.
Variation: Shape dough into rolls. If making rolls reduce the cooking time to 25-30 minutes.

Turkish Flat Bread (pg 126), Mixed Seed Bread, Herbed Beer Bread (pg 127)

Turkish Flat Bread (Pide)

Makes 18 pieces **4g fat per piece**

3¹/₃ cups (500g) plain flour
1 sachet (7g) dry yeast
pinch salt (or salt substitute)
1 teaspoon sugar
1¹/₂ cups warm water
2 tablespoons olive oil
1 egg, lightly beaten
¹/₃ cup sesame seeds (cracked pepper or herbs)

Combine flour, yeast, salt and sugar in a bowl. Make a well in the centre. Stir in water and oil. Mix to make a soft dough. Knead on a lightly floured surface for 10 minutes, adding more flour as needed, until soft, elastic and smooth. Place in a lightly oiled bowl. Turn to coat with oil. Cover. Stand in a warm place for 1 hour or until doubled in size. Punch down. Divide into 2 equal portions. Roll each portion into a ball. Cover with a tea towel. Stand in a warm place for 20-30 minutes. Flatten each ball to make a 25cm circle. Pull into an oval shape. Place on a lightly greased baking tray. Make indentations over surface with fingertips, leaving a 2.5cm border. Brush generously with egg. Sprinkle with sesame seeds. Bake at 220°C for 15 minutes or until golden. Wrap in a tea towel. Cool.

F&P: Can be frozen for up to 2 months.

Seeded Cheese Damper

Makes 12 wedges **3.5g fat per wedge**

2 cups self-raising flour, sifted
1 tablespoon chopped fresh chives
¹/₄ cup sunflower seeds
¹/₂ cup (100g) crumbled reduced-fat and -salt fetta cheese
freshly ground black pepper to taste
1 cup buttermilk
low-fat milk for brushing
1 teaspoon grated Parmesan cheese
1 tablespoon sunflower seeds, extra

Combine flour, chives, ¹/₄ cup sunflower seeds, fetta cheese and pepper in a bowl. Make a well in the centre. Pour in buttermilk. Mix to make a soft dough. Knead on a lightly floured surface into a ball. Place on a lightly greased baking tray. Brush with milk. Sprinkle with Parmesan cheese and remaining sunflower seeds. Bake at 180°C for 45-50 minutes or until golden and base sounds hollow when tapped.

F&P: Can be frozen for up to 1 month. Reheat from frozen at 150°C for 15 minutes.

Raspberry Muffins

Makes 10 muffins **2g fat per muffin**

1 cup wholemeal self-raising flour
1 cup white self-raising flour
¹/₂ cup bran
¹/₂ teaspoon bicarbonate of soda
1 teaspoon ground ginger
³/₄ cup buttermilk
¹/₃ cup orange juice concentrate
2 eggs
²/₃ cup fresh (or frozen, partly thawed) raspberries
1 teaspoon chopped glace ginger

Sift together dry ingredients into a bowl. Return any bran to the bowl. Beat together buttermilk, orange juice and eggs. Pour into dry ingredients, all at once. Add raspberries and ginger. Mix until just combined, take care not to overmix. Spoon into greased muffin pans. Bake at 180°C for 20-25 minutes or until cooked when tested with a skewer.

F&P: Can be frozen for up to 3 months.
Zucchini Poppy Seed Muffins: Omit raspberries and ginger and mix 1 cup grated zucchini and 2 tablespoons poppy seeds into the dry ingredients before adding the liquid.

HERBED BEER BREAD

Makes 16 slices   **3g fat per slice**

2 cups plain flour
1 teaspoon bicarbonate of soda
2 tablespoons grated Parmesan cheese
2 tablespoons chopped pitted black olives
2 tablespoons olive oil
3/4 cup beer, approximately
3/4 cup chopped mixed fresh herbs (e.g.
     parsley, basil, coriander and oregano)
low-fat milk for brushing

Combine flour, bicarbonate of soda, Parmesan cheese and olives in a bowl. Make a well in the centre. Mix in oil and enough beer to make a moist dough. Spoon one-third of the dough into a greased 8 x 20cm loaf pan. Sprinkle with one-half of the herbs. Top with one-third of the remaining dough. Sprinkle with remaining herbs. Top with remaining dough. Brush with milk. Bake at 180°C for 1 hour or until base sounds hollow when tapped.

F&P: Can be frozen for up to 2 months.

Raisin 'n' Cheese Loaf, Seeded Cheese Damper, Corn Bread, Zucchini Poppy Seed Muffins

RAISIN 'N' CHEESE LOAF

Makes 18 slices   **4g fat per slice**

1 1/2 cups raisins, chopped
3/4 cup boiling water
1 3/4 cups self-raising flour
1/2 cup caster sugar
1/2 cup grated low-fat tasty cheese
1/2 cup walnuts, chopped
1 egg, lightly beaten

Place raisins in a bowl. Pour over boiling water. Stand for 5 minutes. Sift together flour and sugar into a bowl. Stir in cheese and walnuts. Add egg and undrained raisin mixture. Stir until well combined. Spoon into a 13 x 21cm loaf pan. Bake at 160°C for 50-60 minutes or until cooked when tested with a skewer. Stand for 5 minutes. Turn onto a wire rack. Cool.

F&P: Can be frozen for up to 3 months.

CORN BREAD

Makes 24 slices   **1.5g fat per slice**

2 cups cornmeal
1/2 cup wheat germ
1/2 teaspoon bicarbonate of soda
1 teaspoon baking powder
1 tablespoon brown sugar
1 large egg
1 tablespoon canola oil
2 cups buttermilk

Combine dry ingredients in a bowl. Mix together wet ingredients. Add to dry ingredients. Mix to combine. Spoon into greased and lined 20cm square cake pan. Bake at 190-200°C for 20-25 minutes or until cooked when tested with a skewer and bread is golden.

F&P: Can be frozen for up to 2 months.

CELEBRATIONS

GLAZED SESAME TURKEY

Serves 10   **8g fat per serve**

5kg turkey, skin and fat removed
3-4 pieces of fresh fruit (e.g. plums, apples,
     apricots and pears)
1 tablespoon olive oil
1 tablespoon honey
1 tablespoon orange juice
1 tablespoon sesame seeds
1 teaspoon reduced-salt soy sauce
1 teaspoon dried oregano
1/4 cup cranberry sauce
1 tablespoon sesame seeds, extra

Fill cavity of turkey with fruit. Place breast side up on a wire rack in a deep baking dish. Pierce flesh several times with a sharp knife. Quarter fill baking dish with water. Combine oil, honey, orange juice, sesame seeds, soy sauce and oregano. Brush over turkey. Cover with a foil tent. Bake at 180°C for 2 hours. Remove foil. Brush turkey with pan juices. Spread with cranberry sauce. Sprinkle with extra sesame seeds. Bake, uncovered, for a 15-30 minutes longer or until cooked. Serve with Wild Rice and Apple Seasoning (this page) and baked vegetables.

Cook's tip: For extra flavour add fresh herbs such as rosemary, thyme or oregano and dry white wine to the water in the baking dish.
Nutrition note: Fat content based on a turkey flesh serve size of 110-150g.

CHRISTMAS FRUITS

allow about 125g mixed fresh fruit per serve
unsweetened fruit juice (e.g. apple or orange)
1 cinnamon stick

Peel fruit. Cut into a variety of shapes. Half fill a saucepan with fruit juice. Add cinnamon stick. Bring to the boil. Poach fruit. Start with the lighter coloured fruit. Most fruit will need about 5 minutes. Remove fruit as it cooks. Drain well. Bring liquid in saucepan to the boil. Boil, uncovered until reduced to a syrup.

Cook's tip: Use fresh fruits such as grapes, tamarillos, figs, blood plums, peaches, pears, pineapple and dates. Choose a variety of colour and flavour combinations. Peaches and pears can be poached in red wine.

WILD RICE AND APPLE SEASONING

Serves 10   **4g fat per serve**

1 tablespoon oil
1 cup finely chopped celery
1 large onion, finely chopped
3 apples, finely chopped
4 cups cooked brown rice and wild rice blend
1 1/2 cups low-salt chicken stock
1/2 cup unsweetened apple juice
1/2 cup raisins
1 teaspoon dried sage
1 teaspoon dried thyme
1/4 teaspoon ground nutmeg
12 slices wholemeal (or cracked wheat) bread,
     cut into 1cm cubes

Heat oil in a non-stick frying pan. Add celery and onion. Cook for 3 minutes. Add apples. Cook for 5 minutes or until tender. Place in a bowl. Mix in remaining ingredients. Spoon onto a baking tray. Cover with foil. Bake for 40 minutes. Remove foil. Bake for 5 minutes longer.

Salsas are a great low-fat option to replace sauces and add colour and flavour boosts to meals. Finely dice fresh vegetables (e.g. tomatoes, cucumber, corn and onion) and a little fruit, if desired, add a splash of balsamic or flavoured vinegar, fruit juice or wine.

Glazed Sesame Turkey, Wild Rice and Apple Seasoning;
Brandy Sauce, Plum Pudding (pg 130), Christmas Fruits

Plum Pudding with Brandy Sauce

Serves 10   **6.5g fat per serve**

250g mixed dried fruit
125g pitted prunes
$1/4$ cup cold tea
1 teaspoon grated lemon rind
$1/4$ cup lemon juice
1 teaspoon mixed spice
$1/2$ teaspoon ground nutmeg
$1/2$ teaspoon ground cinnamon
$1/2$ teaspoon ground ginger
$1/4$ cup brandy
1 cup plain flour
$1/3$ cup brown sugar
1 cup fresh breadcrumbs (preferably made
     from 1-2 day old bread)
$1/2$ teaspoon bicarbonate of soda
2 eggs, lightly beaten
2 tablespoons canola (or vegetable) oil

BRANDY SAUCE

1 egg
1 tablespoon sugar
2 teaspoons plain flour
1 cup hot low-fat milk
2 tablespoons brandy

Combine dried fruit, prunes, tea, lemon rind and juice and spices in a saucepan. Simmer for 3 minutes. Cool. Transfer to a bowl. Add brandy. Cover. Stand overnight.

Combine flour, sugar, breadcrumbs and bicarbonate of soda in a bowl. Add brandied fruit mixture, eggs and oil. Mix well. Pour into a greased pudding basin (about 1 litre capacity). Press mixture down. Cover with non-stick baking paper. Cover loosely with a cloth or foil. Tie securely with string. Place in saucepan of rapidly boiling water (the water should come halfway up sides of basin). Cover. Steam for $3^1/2$ hours. On Christmas day, steam for another $2^1/2$ hours. To serve, turn onto a heated plate. Accompany with Brandy Sauce and Christmas Fruits (pg 128). To flame the pudding, heat a little extra brandy or cognac until it starts to simmer. Pour over pudding. Ignite at the table.

Brandy Sauce: Beat egg, sugar and flour until light and fluffy. Transfer to a saucepan. Gradually stir in hot milk. Bring to the boil, stirring constantly. Reduce heat. Simmer for 1 minute. Remove from heat. Stir in brandy.

Cook's tip: Pudding may be stored after first steaming for several months in a cool, dry place.

Fruit Mince Pies

Makes 24 pies   **7g fat per pie**

1 quantity Sweet Almond Pastry (pg 138)
1 egg white, lightly beaten

FRUIT FILLING

$1/4$ cup mixed peel
$1/4$ cup sultanas
$1/4$ cup raisins
$1/4$ cup currants
$1/4$ cup chopped dried apricots
$1/4$ cup drained, canned crushed unsweetened
     pineapple
1 apple, finely chopped
2 tablespoons finely chopped almonds or
     hazelnuts
1 teaspoon grated lemon rind
1 teaspoon grated orange rind
1 tablespoon orange juice
2 tablespoons brown sugar
1 teaspoon ground cloves
1 teaspoon ground cinnamon
1 teaspoon mixed spice
1 tablespoon rum

Roll out pastry to 3mm thick. Cut pastry into 24 rounds, using a 7.5cm cutter. Cut remaining pastry into decorative shapes or rounds for top of pies. Gently ease pastry rounds into greased patty or muffin pans. Divide filling between pastry cases. Top with decorative shapes. Brush pastry with egg white. Bake at 180°C for 20-25 minutes or until golden.

Filling: Place all ingredients in a bowl. Mix well. Place in an airtight container. Refrigerate for at least 5 days, turning occasionally.

Frozen Christmas Pudding (pg 134), Panforte (pg 133), Marinated Fish and Scallop Kebabs (pg 132), Turkey Pecan Roulade with Cranberry and Orange Salsa (pg 134)

Ricotta Christmas Cake

Makes 96 pieces **1g fat per piece**

1¼ cups (250g) ricotta cheese
1 teaspoon bicarbonate of soda
1.5kg mixed dried fruit
½ cup red glace cherries
¼ cup honey
½ cup blanched almonds
1½ cups unsweetened juice, for example
    dark grape, orange or pineapple
2¾ cups self-raising flour, sifted
½ cup plain wholemeal flour, sifted
2 teaspoons mixed spice
2 tablespoons brandy

Combine ricotta cheese, bicarbonate of soda, fruit, honey, almonds and juice in a saucepan. Simmer for 5 minutes. Cool. Add dry ingredients. Mix well. Stir in brandy. Spoon mixture into a greased and lined 23cm square cake pan. Bake at 160-170°C for 2-2½ hours or until cooked when tested with a skewer. If desired, sprinkle hot cake with extra brandy and wrap in a towel to cool.

Almond Crescents

Makes 20 crescents **7g fat per crescent**

1 egg white
¼ cup sugar
1 tablespoon honey
1 teaspoon grated orange rind
2 cups ground almonds
2 tablespoons self-raising flour
icing sugar for dusting

Beat egg white until soft peaks form. Gradually beat in sugar and honey. Continue beating until sugar dissolves. Combine orange rind, ground almonds and flour. Fold into egg white. Shape dough into finger-sized logs. Shape into crescents. Place on a lightly greased baking tray. Bake at 150°C for 30-40 minutes or until golden. Cool. Lightly dust with sifted icing sugar.

Marinated Fish and Scallop Kebabs

Serves 4 as main meal **7.5g fat per serve**

400g firm fish fillets (e.g. tuna, salmon, ocean
    trout, blue-eye cod, warehou, flake, baramundi
    or Spanish mackerel), cut into 2cm pieces
8 fresh scallops
¼ cup lemon juice
2 tablespoons dry white wine
1 tablespoon olive oil
1 tablespoon grated fresh ginger
freshly black ground pepper to taste
1 tablespoon chopped fresh parsley
1 tablespoon chopped fresh dill (or coriander)

Thread fish onto 8 skewers with a scallop in the centre of each. Combine remaining ingredients. Brush generously over kebabs. Cover. Refrigerate for 1 hour. Barbecue or grill kebabs, brushing with marinade until fish flakes, take care not to overcook. Serve with a salsa of finely chopped mixed capsicum, Spanish (red) onion and cucumber mixed with a little lemon juice or balsamic vinegar.

Baked Rainbow Trout

Serves 4 **16g fat per serve**

1 tablespoon olive oil
juice 1 lemon (or lime)
1 tablespoon chopped fresh ginger
1 tablespoon chopped fresh parsley
freshly ground black pepper to taste
4 small (200g each) rainbow trout
1 lemon, sliced
8 large spinach (or lettuce) leaves

Combine oil, lemon juice, ginger, parsley and pepper. Brush over trout. Place 2 lemon slices in cavity of each trout. Wrap each trout in spinach, then in foil. Bake at 180°C for 15-20 minutes or until flesh just flakes when tested with a fork. Serve with Yoghurt Cucumber Sauce (pg 136).

PANFORTE

Makes 40 wedges   **4.5g fat per wedge**

rice paper
1 cup whole hazelnuts, toasted, skins
    removed, chopped
1 cup blanched almonds, toasted
1 cup mixed peel
120g mixed glace fruit, chopped
1 teaspoon grated lemon rind
$1/2$ cup plain flour
1 teaspoon ground cinnamon
$1/4$ teaspoon ground coriander
$1/4$ teaspoon ground cloves
$1/4$ teaspoon ground nutmeg
pinch ground white pepper
$1/3$ cup sugar
$1/2$ cup honey
icing sugar (optional)

Line base of a 22cm round springform tin
with rice paper.
Combine nuts, mixed peel, glace fruit, lemon
rind, flour and spices in a bowl. Combine
sugar and honey in a saucepan. Stir over low
heat until sugar dissolves, brushing sides of
pan with a brush dipped in hot water to
dissolve all the sugar. Bring to the boil.
Reduce heat. Simmer for 6-8 minutes or until
mixture reaches soft ball stage. Immediately
pour over fruit mixture. Stir quickly to
thoroughly combine. Pour into prepared tin.
Smooth top. Bake at 180°C for 35 minutes.
The panforte won't be coloured or seem
firm, but it hardens as it cools. Cool in pan on
a wire rack. Cut into very thin wedges.
Sprinkle with icing sugar (if using). *Recipe
adapted from Joe Trimboli's Panforte recipe
from Cafe Mezzaluna, Canberra*

Cook's tip: Any variety of glace fruit such as
pineapple, apricots and ginger can be used in
this recipe. Rice paper is available from
supermarkets, health food stores and
delicatessens. Panforte can be stored in an
airtight container for 1-2 months.

Top: Hot Cross Buns (pg 135), Orange Salad (pg 96),
    Baked Rainbow Trout, Greek Easter Bread (pg135)
Almond Crescents, Yoghurt Cucumber Sauce (pg 136)
Bottom: Ricotta Christmas Cake, Fruit Mince Pies (pg 130)

Turkey Pecan Roulade with Cranberry and Orange Salsa

Serves 6   **10g fat per serve**

500g boneless turkey breast

PECAN AND CORNBREAD SEASONING

1 tablespoon olive oil
3 spring onions, chopped
2 teaspoons dried sage
1/2 cup chopped pecans
1/4 loaf Corn Bread (pg 127), crumbled
1/2 cup low-fat milk
frreshly ground black pepper to taste

CRANBERRY AND ORANGE SALSA

1 tablespoon brown sugar
1/4 cup orange juice
2 star anise (optional)
2 cups canned (or frozen) cranberries
    (strawberries or blueberries)
1/4 teaspoon bottled drained pink peppercorns
    (optional)
1 teaspoon grated orange rind
1 orange, segmented

Butterfly turkey breast. Pound until an even thickness. Place on a sheet of foil. Spoon seasoning along centre of turkey. Roll tightly to enclose seasoning. Wrap in foil. Twist ends to seal. Place in a baking dish. Bake at 180°C for 45-60 minutes or until cooked. Stand for 10-15 minutes before carving. Serve with salsa.

Seasoning: Heat oil in a non-stick frying pan. Add onions, sage, pecans and crumbled cornbread. Cook until onions are soft. Remove from heat. Cool slightly. Add milk and pepper. Stir until mixture comes together.

Salsa: Combine sugar, orange juice and star anise (if using) in a small saucepan. Bring to the boil. Reduce heat. Simmer for 5 minutes. Add cranberries. Cook for 10 minutes or until thickened slightly. Cool. Stir in peppercorns (if using), orange rind and segments.

Cook's tip: Drained cranberry sauce can be used instead of canned or frozen cranberries.

Frozen Christmas Pudding

Makes 15 wedges   **10g fat per wedge**

3/4 cup raisins
1/2 cup sultanas
1/3 cup currants
1/2 cup sweet sherry
1/4 cup brandy
3/4 cup glace cherries
1/2 cup mixed peel
1/2 cup glace ginger, chopped
1/2 cup walnuts, chopped
1/2 cup toasted almonds (or hazelnuts),
    chopped,
1 litre low-fat vanilla ice-cream, softened
    slightly
1 litre low-fat chocolate ice-cream, softened
    slightly

Combine raisins, sultanas, currants, sherry and brandy in a bowl. Cover. Soak overnight. Stir in remaining fruit and nuts. Divide mixture in half.

Place vanilla ice-cream in a large bowl. Stir in half of the fruit mixture. Spoon mixture into base of a 8-cup (2 litre) capacity decorative mould. Freeze.

Place chocolate ice-cream in a large bowl. Stir through remaining fruit mixture. Carefully spoon over vanilla ice-cream layer. Cover. Freeze.

To serve, remove pudding from the freezer about 10 minutes before serving. Invert onto a serving platter. Decorate with fresh fruit, angelica or holly, if desired.

Variations: Any glace or dried fruit or nuts can be used in this recipe. For extra colour and interest, add a third layer of low-fat strawberry or cappuccino ice-cream.

HOT CROSS BUNS

Makes 18 buns   **3.5g fat per bun**

3 sachets (7g) dry yeast
1 cup lukewarm low-fat milk
pinch salt
2 tablespoons light brown sugar
1 teaspoon ground cinnamon
$1/2$ teaspoon ground nutmeg
$1/4$ teaspoon ground allspice
2 eggs
4 cups plain flour
2 tablespoons canola (or vegetable) oil
2 tablespoons mixed peel
2 tablespoons sultanas

CROSS
$1/2$ cup plain flour
$1/3$ cup water

GLAZE
$1/2$ teaspoon gelatine
2 tablespoons icing sugar
2 tablespoons warm low-fat milk

Place yeast in a large bowl. Pour in milk. Stand in a warm place for 10 minutes or until frothy. Stir in salt, sugar and spices. Beat in eggs, one at a time. Stir in half the flour to make a soft dough. Beat in oil. Continue beating for 1 minute. Knead in remaining flour. Place dough in a lightly oiled bowl. Turn to coat with oil. Cover with plastic wrap. Stand in a warm place for 1 hour or until doubled in size.

Knead dough, working in mixed peel and sultanas on a lightly floured surface. Roll into a log. Cut into 18 even-sized pieces. Shape pieces into buns. Place buns, 2-3cm apart, on greased baking trays. Cover. Stand in a warm place for 20 minutes. Spoon cross mixture into a piping bag fitted with a small plain nozzle. Mark a cross on top each bun. Bake at 200°C for 15 minutes or until golden. Brush warm buns with glaze.

Cross: Place flour and water in a bowl. Beat until smooth.

Glaze: Place all ingredients in a bowl. Mix until smooth.

GREEK EASTER BREAD

Makes 20 slices   **4g fat per slice**

30g fresh yeast, crumbled
1 cup low-fat milk, warmed
2 tablespoons caster sugar
$3^1/2$ cups plain flour
pinch salt
$1/2$ teaspoon ground nutmeg
$1/2$ teaspoon ground allspice
2 tablespoons canola (or vegetable) oil
2 eggs, lightly beaten
2 teaspoons grated lemon rind
1 egg, lightly beaten, extra
2 tablespoons sesame seeds

Combine yeast, milk and 1 teaspoon each of the sugar and flour in a small bowl. Cover. Stand in a warm place for 10 minutes or until mixture is frothy.

Combine remaining sugar and sifted flour, salt and spices in a large bowl. Add yeast mixture, oil, 2 eggs and lemon rind. Mix to a soft dough. Knead dough on a lightly floured surface for 10 minutes or until smooth. Place in a lightly oiled bowl. Turn to coat with oil. Cover. Stand in a warm place for 1 hour or until dough doubles in size. Punch down. Knead dough on lightly floured surface until smooth. Divide dough into three pieces. Roll each piece to make a 60cm log. Plait logs together. Shape into a ring and pinch ends together to join and seal. Place bread on a lightly greased baking tray. Cover. Stand in a warm place for 40 minutes or until dough is almost doubled in size. Brush with extra egg. Sprinkle with sesame seeds. Bake at 180-190°C for 35-40 minutes or until bread sounds hollow when base is tapped.

Variation: If desired, decorate bread before baking with eggs brushed with edible Greek red dye (available from delicatessens and health food stores).

BASICS

GRILLED VEGETABLES

Many vegetables are suitable for char-grilling. Zucchini, eggplant, capsicum, kumara, mushrooms and pumpkin are all great grilled. Cut vegetables into 5mm thick slices. Lightly brush with olive oil. Cook under a hot grill or on a barbecue until skin blisters or flesh is soft and cooked.

HONEY GINGER SAUCE

Makes about 1 cup   **neg fat**

$^1/_2$ cup orange juice
$^1/_2$ cup water
2 tablespoons honey
1 teaspoon ground ginger
1 teaspoon finely chopped fresh (or glace) ginger
3 teaspoons cornflour

Combine orange juice, $^1/_4$ cup water, honey and ginger in a small saucepan, Cook, stirring, until heated through. Blend cornflour with remaining water. Stir into pan. Cook, stirring, until sauce boils and thickens.

Cook's tip: Suitable for chicken, salmon, tuna and vegetables dishes.

YOGHURT CUCUMBER SAUCE

Makes 2 cups   **neg fat**

$1^1/_2$ cups low-fat natural yoghurt
2 tablespoons finely chopped fresh mint
1 tablespoon finely chopped fresh dill
1 Lebanese cucumber, grated
2 tablespoons lemon (or lime) juice

Place all ingredients in a bowl. Mix well.

Cook's tip: Suitable for grilled fish, vegetables, kebabs and salads.

THOUSAND ISLAND DRESSING

Makes 1 cup   **neg fat**

$^1/_4$ cup no-added-salt tomato juice
$^1/_2$ cup low-fat natural yoghurt
1 tablespoon no-added-salt tomato paste
1 tablespoon lemon juice
$^1/_4$ teaspoon dried chives
1 teaspoon chopped fresh parsley

Place all ingredients in a bowl. Mix well.

TOMATO SAUCE

Make 3 cups   **1.5g fat per $^1/_4$ cup**

810g canned no-added-salt tomatoes (or 800g very ripe fresh tomatoes, peeled and diced)
1 tablespoon extra virgin olive oil
1 clove garlic, finely chopped
1 onion, finely chopped
1 tablespoon no-added-salt tomato paste
$^1/_2$ teaspoon sugar
freshly ground black pepper to taste
1 tablespoon chopped fresh basil (or 1 teaspoon dried basil)
1 tablespoon chopped fresh parsley

Puree tomatoes in a food processor. Push through a sieve. Discard seeds. Heat oil in a saucepan. Add garlic. Cook until fragrant. Add onion. Cook until soft. Add pureed tomatoes, tomato paste, sugar and pepper. Bring to the boil. Reduce heat. Simmer for 20 minutes. Add basil and parsley. Simmer for 5-10 minutes or until sauce thickens slightly. Serve immediately, or cool at room temperature. Cover. Store in the refrigerator.

Cook's tip: Suitable for pastry dishes, rice, pasta, grilled meat and chicken or use as a base for sauces and casseroles.

WALNUT SAUCE

Makes 1 cup   11g fat per 2 tablespoons

1/2 cup low-salt chicken stock
1/2 onion, finely chopped
1 clove garlic, crushed
1 teaspoon paprika
1/4 cup red wine vinegar
2 tablespoons chopped fresh coriander
100g finely chopped (or ground) walnuts

Place all ingredients in a food processor. Process to combine.

Cook's tip: Suitable for vegetables and fish.

CREAMY STYLE DRESSING

Makes 2 cups   1.5g fat per 2 tablespoons

3/4 cup (150g) ricotta cheese
200g low-fat natural yoghurt
1/4 cup red wine vinegar
fresh herbs or seasoning (e.g. mustard,
    tarragon, parsley, pepper, chives)

Puree ricotta cheese in food processor. Add yoghurt and vinegar. Process until well combined. Transfer to a bowl. Stir in seasonings.

Cook's tip: Suitable for coleslaw, potato salad, rice and pasta salad.

BALSAMIC DRESSING

Makes 1/3 cup   5g fat per tablespoon

1/4 cup balsamic vinegar
1 tablespoon olive oil
1 teaspoon wholegrain mustard
freshly ground black pepper to taste

Place all ingredients in a jar. Shake well.

Cook's tip: Suitable for Greek and Italian green and garden salads, warm meat salads and grilled fish, chicken and vegetables.

STOCK

Makes 4 cups   1g fat per cup

2 teaspoons vegetable oil
1 onion, chopped
1 stick celery with leaves, chopped
1 large carrot, chopped
1/2 leek, white only, chopped
700g-1kg chicken, turkey, beef or veal bones,
    skin and fat removed
1.25 litres water
1 bay leaf
4 sprigs fresh parsley
2 sprigs fresh thyme
1/4 teaspoon whole black peppercorns
2 cloves

Heat oil in a large saucepan. Add onion, celery, carrot and leek. Cook for 2 minutes. Add bones, water, bay leaf, parsley, thyme, peppercorns and cloves. Bring to the boil, skimming any foam that rises to the surface. Reduce heat. Cover. Simmer for 4-5 hours for chicken and turkey; 6-7 hours for beef and veal. Adding more water if necessary. Strain stock. Cool. Cover. Refrigerate until well chilled. Skim any fat from the surface.

Cook's tip: Stock can be frozen for up to 6 months. This recipe can also be used to make fish stock. Decrease the cooking time for fish stock to 20 minutes. Fish stock should only be frozen for 2-3 weeks. For convenience, freeze stock in ice-cube trays, use a cube of stock instead of oil or margarine in stir-fries, soups and casseroles.

Lemon Yoghurt Icing

Makes ¹/₂ cup   **neg fat**

1 cup icing sugar, sifted
1 tablespoon low-fat natural yoghurt
¹/₂ teaspoon finely grated lemon rind
¹/₂ teaspoon lemon juice

Place all ingredients in a bowl or food processor. Blend until smooth.

Cook's tip: Suitable for cakes, slices and muffins. Store, covered, in the refrigerator for up to 5 days.

Ricotta Pastry

2 cups self-raising flour
2 tablespoons vegetable oil
³/₄ cup (150g) ricotta cheese
¹/₄ cup low-fat milk
1 egg white

Place all the ingredients in a food processor. Process using the pulse button or lightly mix with a knife until pastry just comes together. Add a little cold water if pastry is too dry. Press pastry into a ball. Wrap in plastic wrap. Refrigerate for at least 30 minutes before using.

Sweet Almond Pastry

1¹/₃ cups plain flour
²/₃ cup self-raising flour
2 tablespoons cornflour
1¹/₄ cups ground almonds
3 teaspoons icing sugar
60g poly/monounsaturated margarine
1 egg, lightly beaten
¹/₃ cup iced water, approximately

Combine flours, almonds and sugar in a bowl. Rub in margarine until mixture resembles fine breadcrumbs. Stir in egg and enough water to make ingredients just come together. Knead on a floured surface until smooth. Wrap in plastic wrap. Refrigerate for at least 30 minutes before using.

"A recipe is not meant to be followed exactly . . . it is a canvas on which to embroider, improvise and invent."

Roger Verge 1979

MEASURES & CONVERSIONS

METRIC CUP AND SPOON SIZES

Measures used in this book refer to the standard metric cup and spoon sets approved by Standards Australia.

A basic metric cup set consists of 1 cup, ½ cup, ⅓ cup and ¼ cup sizes. The basic spoon set comprises 1 tablespoon, 1 teaspoon, ½ teaspoon and ¼ teaspoon.

Cup	Spoon
¼ cup = 60 ml	¼ teaspoon = 1.25 ml
⅓ cup = 80 ml	½ teaspoon = 2.5 ml
½ cup = 125 ml	1 teaspoon = 5 ml
1 cup = 250 ml	1 tablespoon = 20 ml

MASS (weight)
(Approximate conversions for cookery purposes)

Imperial	Metric	Imperial	Metric
½ oz	15 g	10 oz	315 g
1 oz	30 g	11 oz	345 g
2 oz	60 g	12 oz (¾ lb)	375 g
3 oz	90 g	13 oz	410 g
4 oz (¼ lb)	125 g	14 oz	440 g
5 oz	155 g	15 oz	470 g
6 oz	185 g	16 oz (1 lb)	500 g (0.5 kg)
7 oz	220 g	24 oz (1½ lb)	750 g
8 oz (½ lb)	250 g	32 oz (2 lb)	1000 g (1 kg)
9 oz	280 g	3 lb	1500 g (1.5 kg)

LIQUIDS

Imperial	Cup	Metric
1 fl oz		30 ml
2 fl oz	¼ cup	60 ml
3 fl oz		100 ml
4 fl oz	½ cup	125 ml
5 fl oz (½ pint)		150 ml
6 fl oz	¾ cup	200 ml
8 fl oz	1 cup	250 ml
10 fl oz (½ pint)	1¼ cups	300 ml
12 fl oz	1½ cups	375 ml
14 fl oz	1¾ cups	425 ml
15 fl oz		475 ml
16 fl oz	2 cups	500 ml
20 fl oz (1 pint)	2½ cups	600 ml

	Fahrenheit	Celsius
Very slow	250°	120°
Slow	275-300°	140-150°
Moderately slow	325°	160°
Moderate	350°	180°
Moderately hot	375°	190°
Hot	400-450°	200-230°
Very hot	475-500°	250-260°

INDEX

PICK THE TICK

When shopping for food look for the Heart Foundation's Tick of Approval (below). The Tick makes healthy food choices quick and easy, and you can be sure a product with the Tick meets the Heart Foundation nutrition guidelines.

The Tick is on all kinds of food products, including some that may surprise you. For example, it's on foods high in fat, such as margarines, oils and nuts. That's because the type of fat in these products is better than others.

Margarines and oils with the Tick contain the healthier types of fats that help to lower high blood cholesterol. You'll even find the Tick on some treats like ice-cream and meat pies that have less total fat, saturated fat and/or salt than usual products of that kind. But it's important to remember that all fats – even those with the Tick – are high in calories and should only be eaten in small amounts.

HOW DOES THE TICK WORK?

Companies apply to put the Tick on their products, but only products which pass strict independent tests to ensure they meet the Heart Foundation's guidelines are permitted to display it.

Companies pay a licence fee to use the Tick. The Heart Foundation is a non-profit charity, and without these fees it would not be able to educate people about the Tick, support national nutrition research and education programs, and run the Pick the Tick program.

HEART FOUNDATION STATE DIVISION OFFICES

NEW SOUTH WALES
Sydney: 4/407 Elizabeth St, Surry Hills NSW 2010
Ph: (02) 9219 2444
Newcastle: Suite 5, OTP House, Bradford Close,
Kotara NSW 2289 Ph: (02) 4952 4699

QUEENSLAND
Brisbane: 557 Gregory Tce, Fortitude Valley QLD 4006
Ph: (07) 3854 1696
Rockhampton: 39 Gladstone Rd, Rockhampton QLD 4700
Ph: (07) 4922 2195
Toowoomba: 417 Ruthven St, Toowoomba QLD 4350
Ph: (07) 4632 3673
Townsville: 36 Gregory St, Townsville QLD 4810
Ph: (07) 4721 4686

SOUTH AUSTRALIA
Adelaide: 155-159 Hutt St, Adelaide SA 5000
Ph: (08) 8224 2888

AUSTRALIA CAPITAL TERRITORY
Canberra: Cnr Denison St & Geils Crt, Deakin ACT 2600
Ph: (02) 6282 5744

TASMANIA
Hobart: 86 Hampden Rd, Battery Point, Hobart TAS 7000
Ph: (03) 6224 2722

VICTORIA
Melbourne: 411 King St, West Melbourne VIC 3003
Ph: (03) 9329 8511

WESTERN AUSTRALIA
Perth: 334 Rokeby Rd, Subiaco WA 6008
Ph: (08) 9388 3343

NORTHERN TERRITORY
Darwin: Third Floor, Darwin Central Building,
21 Knuckey St, Darwin, NT 0800
Ph: (08) 8981 1966

Donation Line: 1300 30 11 65
Heartline 1300 36 27 87
www.heartfoundation.com.au